THE SCALES OF LOVE

PRAISE FOR "THE SCALES OF LOVE"

"Fascinating and compelling! A relevant and engaging must read for men and women."

- Kim Brooks, Bestselling Author of, *She That Findeth*, and *He's Fine...But is He Saved?*

"I am not a big reader, but once I started reading this book, I could not put the book down."

- Dionnedra Reid, *E.M.M.A. Association*

"A powerful, contemporary story! I highly recommend reading with a relevancy that all should read and relate too."

- Sylvia Hubbard, *Motown Writers Network*

"This book absolutely delivers the goods. It's an engaging, relevant and powerful story that everyone needs to read. Once I picked it up, I couldn't put it down until I finished with it."

- Travis Brown, *Business Coach/Entrepreneur*

"After reviewing the manuscript I found it to be intriguing and divine. Experiences and valuable life lessons displayed gives one soul searching tactics to follow. The spiritual aspect assisted in the lesson and held my interest. In my opinion this manuscript is a page turner and I would read again."

- Darnell Glover, Author of, *"Relationships" A Two-Way Street*

"Ladies, this is not just an awesome book. It gives you the opportunity to look at what you allow in your life...good read!"

-Jeannie Simpson, *Motivational/Inspirational Coach*

"I absolutely loved this book. This is a highly recommended read for both males and females. Everyone would be able to relate to the characters in some form."

- Sonya Anthony, *Entrepreneur*

"Overall, The Scales of Love is a compelling and inspiring story of overcoming, forbidden love, self-discovery and God's true design for relationships and why."

- Sabrina Adams, Publisher, *Zoe Life Publishing*

"I have to tell you--I thoroughly enjoyed the book! It was/is so timely and definitely a word in season. I hope you tell the other girls' stories in books of their own--it's just like you said, "...if God isn't in the relationship (the three-fold chord) then we give the devil free range to test us on every level." Thank you for writing the truth in such a very real way, with real characters who are human in every way and with a story that shows how we can meet God wherever we are and HE IS THERE!"

- Sincerely, Cxandra, *Freelance Writer*

THE SCALES OF LOVE

The Battle and Differences of Love

BARAKAH MILLER

GCG INTERNATIONAL

The Scales of Love
Copyright © 2015 Barakah Miller

All rights reserved. No part of this book may be reproduced, distributed or transmitted in any form by any means, graphics, electronics, or mechanical, including photocopy, recording, taping, or by any information storage or retrieval system, without permission in writing from the publisher, except in the case of reprints in the context of reviews, quotes, or references.

This is a work of fiction, inspired by experiences of the author. Any references or similarities to actual events, real people, living or dead, or to real locales are intended to give the novel a sense of relevancy. Any similarity in names, characters, places, events, and incidents is entirely coincidental.

Published by: Barakah Unlimited, LLC

Printed in the United States of America
ISBN-13: 978-0-692-50474-1

Interior Layout & Design: Purposely Created Publishing
www.publishyourgift.com

Model on cover: Mario Duane
www.marioduane/facebook.com
www.marioduane/twitter.com

For information logon to:
info@barakahmiller.com
www.BarakahMiller.com

Dedication

This book is dedicated to all women who have that little girl hidden deep inside of them that has been abandoned, hurt and neglected.

The little girls that lived without love, without the guidance of a father, and was cursed from generations preceding them.

I pray that my journey to finding love within myself encourages you to seek the comfort of God to discover and embrace love for yourself.

I pray you are able to move forward securely in releasing that little girl inside who is waiting to discover her true value and worth.

May the love, joy, peace and wisdom of God lead you to His throne of restoration and deliverance.

TABLE OF CONTENTS

Endorsements	ii
Dedication	vii
Acknowledgements	xi
A Love Memoir	1
Introduction	3
Prologue	5
Chapter 1 Sista Love	7
Chapter 2 Facing the Past	13
Chapter 3 The Return of the Mac	21
Chapter 4 Rekindling the Flame	27
Chapter 5 I Got This!	39
Chapter 6 Following Your Heart	45
Chapter 7 A Love Jones	55
Chapter 8 High off Love	65
Chapter 9 The Balancing Act	75
Chapter 10 Getting the Right Perspective	85
Chapter 11 Time Out for Love	95
Chapter 12 Taking Control	101

TABLE OF CONTENTS

Chapter 13	Embracing Brayla................	109
Chapter 14	Accepting Accountability.........	115
Chapter 15	A Heavy Heart..................	123
Chapter 16	Taking Care of Business..........	129
Chapter 17	Family First.....................	137
Chapter 18	Morning Shuffle.................	143
Chapter 19	Hoop Dreams...................	151
Chapter 20	Love Tested....................	157
Chapter 21	Truth Therapy..................	163
Chapter 22	Love Therapy...................	171
Chapter 23	The Truth Comes Out...........	177
Chapter 24	Learning to Forgive..............	191

Epilogue....................................... 199
What About Me (GOD)......................... 201
5 Things Needed in Order for Your Relationship to Survive..................................... 202
Final Thoughts from the Author................ 203
About the Author.............................. 205

Acknowledgements

To My Children:

I love you all more than words can express. You are my pride and joy...the best thing that has ever happened to me. You all have taught me so much about love; I'm honored to be your mother! Through my own personal journey and experiences, it is my prayer that you all live a full life of love, bliss, and happiness within your own personal intimate relationship.

I love you babes!

To My Heavenly Father:

Words cannot express the love and gratitude I have for you. You have given me so much and have brought me through so many journeys. You have tested my faith and challenged me to believe in myself and you. You have called me into ministry to a higher level than I would have ever imagined. Your trust and faith in me is matchless. I am truly nothing without you and your guidance! I love you Daddy! You are my everything! I would not have become the woman you purposed me to be without this journey.

The Scales of Love

> "God is the God of all comfort in those moments when you want to turn back to that old habit, that old way of thinking which pulls you off track; turn to God and say, 'God, give me your comfort.'" – Anonymous

To My Readers:

It is my desire that you will be inspired to embrace and value who you are as a woman. Dig deep within your soul to acknowledge the worth within your heart and yourself as the beautiful woman that God created you to be. I encourage you to never settle for anything less than your worth! Never allow any relationship or man to compromise your beliefs or consume so much of you that you lose sight of who you are and where your life priorities should be.

When entering a relationship remember to ask yourself: "Are my wants in alignment with my worth?"

I thank you for the support and choosing my book to transform your life. May the love of God bless you richly!

- Barakah

"Transcending Hearts & Minds Through Style & Grace"

Inspired by a True Story

A Love Memoir

I've been thinking about the way we love,

Through distance, time, and patience.

My love for you has evolved passionately and intensely,

That I not only love you...I'm in love with you.

I cannot ignore my heart and just listen to my mind.

Am I loving you blindly – For seeing something inside you that no one else can see?

Long nights, days, hours, minutes and seconds gone by;

Where is my love I so passionately crave?

My mind diverting my heart, denying the love I feel.

Blocked communication suffocates our efforts - could it be divine intervention-

That keeps my true love at a distance?

Forget the rules and the game –

Love, real authentic pure love is not sought or based on mind playing.

I know it looks like I've gone crazy at times and I'm changing.

The Scales of Love

But in the way of love inseparable is how we should be.

I'll be crazy for us; I carry your heart within the depths of my soul.

Forever I will love you, so call me insane, call me a fool.

Tell me that loving you the way I do, it's ridiculous.

I don't mind 'cause loving you is a perfect way to spend a lifetime!

Introduction

You can close your eyes to the things you do not want to see, but you cannot close your heart to the things you do not want to feel.
- Anonymous

So here I am 35 years later with the only vivid memory of my father is watching him walk out the door without any type of explanation or goodbye. Traumatized by my father's abandonment and left with emotions of neglect, fear, unworthiness, pain, and no daddy to love me or ever any hope of being 'daddy's little girl' has left me empty with a replay of unhealthy relationships going nowhere but down 'used and taken for granted' street. I was clueless on what having a sustainable relationship meant let alone how to maintain one...oh and at the thought of love entering the picture, I either ran from it, sabotaged it or allowed fear to overtake me that I ended up doing something to push the poor guy away.

Never did I realize my future will be so jacked up over my father's absence or him leaving my mother and me. Guess no matter how successful you become the demons will show up just to remind you what you have lingering in your closet of unresolved issues. And I must admit my skeletons have definitely been torturing me lately.

The Scales of Love

I'm a well-established business woman with the presumption to have it all together as a single mother. I must say, I do dress it up however, what you get on the outside is not exactly how it appears on the inside. I have two beautiful children who are my world; Dj and Symone. Dj is my little gentleman and protector...the 'man' of the house. And my Symone, she's the sweetest! A true imitation of me, so you probably guessed my concerns with her - unanswered questions, her fears, her struggles, her desire for her Daddy, and unanswered questions to be resolved just as I once longed for.

I struggle with revealing the truth to my little angel. Ashamed and embarrassed of the nature of my relationship with her father and how the truth will affect Symone, slowly kills me inside. Never considering the consequences of my actions in the midst of it all until the moment I saw Symone precious face.

I have got to get back to Brayla and in the process re-evaluate 'Are my Wants in Alignment with my Worth?"

Prologue

Have you ever felt the pain of rejection, even though you didn't want what you were losing? - Lisa Nichols

It's Friday on a warm summer evening. Brayla is playing in her room when all of sudden, she hears her parents, Joseph and Babette, arguing. As their voices become louder, Brayla moves into the hallway and sees her mother standing in her bedroom, crying and yelling at her father as he turns away and proceeds to the stairs with his bags in tote. As Babette runs behind Joseph in desperation with tears streaming down her face, she screams in a desperate spite of pain for Joseph not to leave. Joseph opens the front door just as Brayla reaches the top of the stairs. Was he going to leave without an explanation or even a goodbye? He looked up long enough to make eye contact with Brayla, and quickly walked out the door.

1

Sista Love

Some of the most sacred female relationships are the ones you share with your beloved sister, whether blood related or not. There's no bond like a Sista's -cherish it!

It was a Saturday afternoon. Brayla and her home girls Nia, Sasha and Amerus were enjoying an afternoon girl-time brunch. Nia, a remarried divorcee' who is raising her twin niece and nephew in addition to her son is a saved entrepreneur. A former NFL wifey, she is currently married to her high-school bestie, James. Sasha's the sharp, fierce one who is also married with three kids. Sasha is a handle-her-business, no-time-for-yo-mess type of chick! Her boo, Lonzo, is a successful businessman in sports and entertainment. Amerus is the young diva of the mix. Serving as somewhat of a mentee, she's fresh outta college and handles her business, yet she can't seem to balance her career and love life. Then there's me, Brayla, I'm single with two kids and fresh out of a relationship. The thing is my heart is still taken by my ex, Bishop. Even though I'm a successful businesswoman, with three prominent businesses, I

The Scales of Love

still struggle with trying to get this man out of my heart. It's easier said than done for most women, I know. But nonetheless, I'm productive. I take care of my home, have the best home girls a friend could ask for, I love the Lord and I give to my community often. I've mastered applying all the right things to my life – but this one relationship has taken me off course.

Bishop is in upper management at a prominent company. He's in a relationship or, should I say, married with four kids and has been with the same woman since college. His tall, athletic physique makes him more than charming. He's gentle, well-kept, and has the pearls (smile) any woman would want to keep close to her heart. Oh, and his skin is the smoothest, softest, luscious carmelicious texture ever embraced.

I love my girls, but they have no idea that Bishop had a separate life all those years that we were together. Except Nia. I can depend on Nia not to judge, plus she's been through hell and back. Remember, she's a former wifey of an NFL player, so I can only imagine what her ex did to her. Plus, her faith is unshakeable and I know she can guide me through her wisdom from God and life experiences.

You can't share everything with all of your friends. You gotta have discernment and know what and who to share certain information with. Nothing personal. Just wisdom. Plus, you don't want everybody in your mix. They get too hype and can give you the wrong advice. Gotta know the different personalities of your home girls and inner circle. That way, you know what information to share and not to share. Hopefully, they're mature enough to handle and respect your privacy.

"So Brayla, what's really up with you and Bishop?" Sasha asked. "Girl, I know it's been a while since ya'll last talked. But, neither one of you ever said it was officially over."

"Sasha!" Brayla exclaimed. "That's a subject I really don't care to talk about. Besides, knowing Bishop, he probably thinks he can just waltz his behind right back into my life as if no time has gone by and everything is all good. As if there is no work to be put in. I do know that I'm not about to chase him down. He's very much aware of where I reside and how to reach me, if he so desires. I'm not a man chaser. I'm the cake and he's just the frosting in the middle."

"Dang, what about the top of the cake?" Amerus chuckled.

"Girl, please! It takes a whole lot more than what he was willing to give to make it to the top! I don't have to ride any man to get his attention. I refuse!" Brayla bellowed.

"Amen, to that!" Amerus shouted. "And why should we?! I'm just saying."

The Scales of Love

Nia chimed in, "Girl, I'm with you on that. But, let's keep it real...I mean seriously have any of you ever asked yourself the question, "Are your wants in alignment with your worth?" before jumping the gun and getting all emotionally attached? We as women have to remember to be true to ourselves and not to get so wrapped up in any man where we lose ourselves. Don't get so caught up in living his life that you forget you have one of your own."

"Nia, you always share so much wisdom. We also need to make sure we uplift each other and pray for our men, even at times when it's challenging and we don't want to," Brayla explained.

"Oh, shoot," Sasha said. "Listen to Ms. Brayla over there preachin'!"

"Girl, please! Don't act brand new. Seriously," Brayla continued. "If I knew me and Bishop would end like this, I woulda paid more attention instead of listening to my heart."

"See, that's our problem, right there," Amerus said. "We invest too much and end up with nothing in the end. We allow our heart to be so consumed with love that we fail to pay attention to all the signs. I'm young, but that's a lesson I learned early."

Sasha agreed. "But even though we do all that, sometimes we can't help who our heart chooses to love."

"Yeah," Brayla chimed in. "But I wonder how much of that is true. They say 'can't choose who you love' or as Bishop says, 'can't control who your heart chooses to love.' Same thing. But it's kinda contradictory. I mean, we are responsible for our choices, so how can those statements be true? Don't we choose who we want to be with, who we love?"

"Hmmm...that's deep!" Nia shared. "Well, love is deep. In any relationship, you have to have resilience 'cause love will test you and only the strong survive."

"Whew!" Brayla hailed. "Not only that, love has so many elements--loyalty, trust, communication, consistency, oh and giving! As Bishop Murphy says, "There is no indication of love until giving takes place."

In unison, they declare, "Amen to that!"

"Oh," Nia reminded, "Let's not forget love gives, and lust takes!"

"Yes, yes," says this smooth, yet soft baritone voice as Nia, Sasha and Amerus look up. Brayla stared straight with a blank look on her face as Bishop smiled and said, "Good afternoon ladies, Brayla!"

2

Facing the Past

Just when you think you put the past behind, it has a way of showing up at the wrong dang time.

Bishop's abrupt appearance rushed Brayla and the girls off as Bishop persistently tried to communicate with Brayla. Brayla walked toward valet in agitation. As Sasha and Amerus drove off, Brayla and Nia stood waiting on valet to bring them Brayla's car.

In an infuriating tone, Brayla said, "Girl, I can't believe him! I don't know what to feel. How he just gonna pop up at our table, all smooth and debonair like everything's ok?"

"Girl, don't let him steal your joy," Nia said. "Dismiss it like his presence didn't make a difference and you're not bothered by his unannounced appearance."

As valet arrived with Brayla's car, Bishop walked up behind her. "Let me get that for you."

As he opened her car door, Brayla got in. Bishop smiled and said, "It was great seeing you, Brayla."

The Scales of Love

Brayla looked sideways at Bishop, closed her car door and drove off.

Brayla reminded Nia, "Six months girl. Six months, and he thinks he can just waltz his behind back into my life?! Seriously? Ugh!"

"Calm down, girl," Nia said. "I know you're emotional, upset and want to go deep on him, but exhale. Focus. Play your cards right. He's just tryna feel you out to see if he can get back in. Girl, don't play his game and definitely don't pay him any attention. I promise the chase will begin – but don't let him back in if that's what you want. Listen. Be honest with yourself and how you truly feel about him. I know it's been six months, but your feelings may be suppressed. It's okay, girl. Take ownership of those feelings and embrace your relationship, keeping in mind the cost that comes with it. Ask yourself if it's worth it. Be up front with him and set your boundaries. Girl, God's gotcha boo."

"You're right, I can handle this. Greater is He that is in me than he that is in the world. I'm strong. I got this," Brayla confirmed, reassuring herself.

"Just remember, a guilty conscience doesn't need an introduction. A relationship is either going in two directions – marriage or a break-up. You meet a person to get to know them and once you know it's not going anywhere and neither one of you are growing, then somebody needs to be bold enough to end it. But if you don't say anything and he knows you're there and you don't put a demand on him, he'll continue to flow with you until...you're not his booty call! You're making it easy for him to expect so much and give so little."

"Sometimes, being beautiful can be a blessing or a curse. You become immune to the pain and rejection. You build this wall of security to protect your heart and all men become the same. You keep your guard up, and you're always armed and ready. Most people don't recognize the defense mechanism. It takes someone who really has good intentions to see the charade and see past all the hurt and your insecurities. To be honest, his disappearing acts remind me of my father. How can someone who claims they love you just up and leave you? Feeling confused and abandoned without any explanation of what's going on with them? This can't be love, but my heart is so committed to him."

Brayla pulled up in front of Nia's house. They hugged and Nia said, "He knows what he is doing. He has never been willing to terminate his relationship with his wife. Not saying that you have ever asked him to. I just want you to be very informed of your choice and know you have options. I'll call you later, girl."

Brayla drove off in deep thought about Bishop's unannounced appearance. "Lord, this cannot be happening to me. I can't believe this dude. After all this time, he wants

The Scales of Love

to make himself noticeable. Why? What could Mr. Bishop Moore have up his sleeve? Lord, protect me and shield me for what's about to come, in Jesus' name, Amen! I guess the time is coming for the truth to come out. Lord, help me and strengthen me."

Thinking back to when Bishop and I first began developing our relationship, I was so hesitant. I should have stuck to my guns, but the look in his eyes when he realized I intentionally had shown no interest and had not entertained the thought of returning any of his calls was a Kodak moment. The look on his face was priceless! So that evening, I sent him the first of many texts to follow, wishing him safe travels. Amazed, but not fully surprised of his response, "You just made my day. I will definitely keep in touch. As crazy as it seems, I couldn't stop lookin' at you in your eyes or thinkin' about you. I hope you don't think bad of me. Hope you got home safe, too."

The very next day, bright and early, my phone lit up with text messages from him, from 'good morning beautiful' to 'I hope you're having an amazing day...I'll call later.' I must admit, they were beginning to be a little bit annoying. He had officially became my bugaboo! All jokes aside, I explained to him that we could be no more than friends.

His reply was, "A friendship with you is more than enough. I just want to get to know you. I think you're a real cool person, that's all."

"Yeah right," I said. "Bishop seriously, what's your target?"

"I have none really. I just think you're beautiful, that's all! A friendship with you is more than enough for me. I wouldn't have it any other way. And no, I didn't think I would hear from you. Glad though, you seem so cool to be around. Talk to you soon sweetie. Goodnight!"

Bishop pressed in hard for weeks, even after I told him to stop communicating with me. I think he only heard my 'not interested' as a 'yes' and it just made him more persistent. My phone was like clockwork. From 8 a.m. to midday to late in the evening, Bishop made sure that he was not far from my thoughts.

"Hey cutie! Just thinkin' about you. How's your day goin'? Have I crossed your mind any? · Just curious to know."

Could this dude be serious?! Does he have a hearing problem or is he just afraid to accept rejection?

Finally, I screamed, "BISHOP! Stop! Have you paid attention to anything I've said or texted over the last six weeks?"

"Yes, I have," Bishop replied. "I just would like to get to know you, no other intentions...really! I'm a big flirt obviously, and I think you're very attractive. But my comments

The Scales of Love

are only intended to brighten up your day a little, not do anything more. Who really has control over who stays on their mind anyway? Am I starting to bother you for real?"

"What? Is he for real," Brayla said to herself. "Dude," I explained in the calmest voice, "I've been telling you for weeks I'm not interested and to stop all communication. But you must be a little slow because you have not respected my wishes. What's up with you?"

"Okay, Brayla. I get it. I'll stop. I still think you're sexy as heck though. ·" Bishop added.

Brayla laughed to herself.

Later that evening, Bishop convened with his family for their annual family reunion. The life of the party, so to speak, is his manta as he mingles with his family enjoying the festivities. Nyla, his wife, is petite, gorgeous, in love with God and has a career in Business Administration. She's been in love with Bishop since college and four kids later, he is still the love of her life. They were together eight years before getting married and are now on the brink of their 18-year anniversary.

Barakah Miller

She's in love with him and he's in love with her. They are the ideal couple for the romantic at heart; a love to be admired by family and friends. Bishop's children adore him and he is passionate about his kids. However, Nyla has no clue about her husband's unfaithful activities, nor would she ever conceive Bishop to dishonor their vows.

Bishop loves his wife and children. But he has become smitten by Brayla Thompson, a woman he can't seem to shake for whatever reason, the one who has captured his heart. His love for her has become intense and he finds that he has to put his feelings in perspective in order to find balance between his wife and Brayla.

3

The Return of the Mac

Just when you think love has found a new home, it finds its way back on your door step.

It's Sunday, the sun is shining, and Bishop Murphy was on point with the word this morning. My 'angels' are more beautiful with each day! Oh, how I love my babies. Lord, you have truly blessed me –thank you!" exclaimed Brayla. The phone rang and it was Nia.

"Hello, hey girl! How's your Sunday?"

"Brayla, girl you were on my mind this morning in service. Just had to give you a jingle to see how you're doing."

"Nia, girl it's all good. I'm not trippin' off that, Bishop – whatever!"

"That's my girl," Nia shouted. "Well let me get dinner started. We'll chat later."

"Ok, enjoy the fam," Brayla said.

The Scales of Love

Shortly after Bishop and I met, we dated off and on over a course of six years before our recent separation, which ended after eight months from our last breakup. This was a mutual, yet emotional time for me. I never told Bishop, but I was three months pregnant when we separated. Two months later, I met someone and we dated for a year before he got deported to Germany. It didn't matter to him that I was expecting. We never talked about Bishop – in fact, everyone assumed my baby was his because we were together. Five months later, Bishop and I got back together before our last separation. I never told Bishop about my pregnancy to this day. I think about it every time I look into my baby's eyes. I figured things are good the way they are. Why bring it up? I know he has a right to know, so don't judge me. But, we came close before and his response was, "I don't need that kind of stress in my life, ever!"

That's what most men say when they know they have to explain a child to another woman. It's funny though, in the heat of the moment 'stress' is far from the mind as he's screaming out your name!

We'll cross that bridge if and when we get there. Ironically, when we got back together, he never put two and two together or I guess he never really looked my baby in the face long enough to question anything. Who does that after a short term breakup – not count up the months or at least bring it to the table for discussion? I guess he must have been focused on what was in front of him on the real home front, or he just didn't want to know.

He was a little taken back that I had another baby, but he never made it seem as if it was a major concern. Could it have been that he already knew? Maybe he was just afraid to ask a question that he really didn't want an answer to.

"Mom," DJ yelled.

"Yes babe."

"I'm about to take Symone to the park."

"Ok, be careful and make sure you keep your eyes on her!"

"Yes ma'am," DJ said.

As Brayla looked out her bedroom window to watch her kids, a car pulled up outside her house. She moved in closer to the window and to her surprise, it was Bishop.

"Oh, heck naw! I just know he didn't just pull a pop up," she mumbled.

Bishop got out of his car and proceeded to walked up to Brayla's front door. Before he could make it to the driveway, Brayla greeted him from the garage.

"Bishop?" Brayla blurted out in a stern voice, trying to act surprised. "What are you doing here?"

The Scales of Love

"Well a happy Sunday to you as well," Bishop said. "I was out enjoying the day and you came across my mind and so, here I am."

"You don't have those privileges anymore," Brayla reminded him. "Honestly Bishop, what do you want?"

"Why you gotta be so mean Brayla, and why do I have to want something? Brayla, it was just really good seeing you the other day, even though it was for a moment. I miss you. I want you back in my life."

"Ha..." Brayla said to herself. "Even if it's for a little while. Bishop, please. Seriously, we can't do us again. You're married, in case you forgot."

"Brayla, stop! You honestly can look me in the eye and tell me that you don't feel the same? My love for you is real and when I saw you, it all came back. I love you Bray. Why can't you see that?"

"If you can use the L word as loosely as you have with me, then it's true...love is not the opposite of hate. Selfishness is. I think you should leave now," Brayla said, in an uncomfortable tone.

"For real Brayla! Wow. I guess you're not going to answer my question?"

"Bishop, your wife is calling..."

Barakah Miller

"Oh so you got jokes, Brayla? Alright I'll leave. But I meant what I said."

Brayla stood silently as she watched Bishop walk to his car. In her mind, she said, "Lord, help me for what I'm feeling. Give me strength to overcome. Bishop's always been on point in reading me. I pray he's lost his touch."

Brayla's mind flashed back to when Bishop and she first met. It was at a business networking function given by one of Brayla's businesses. Bishop was in conversation when Brayla approached his table to greet everyone. He was taken aback at how stunningly beautiful Brayla was. Her presence was a ray of light. His eyes lit up and his smile was as high as a mountaintop!

"Hello, I'm Bishop Moore. It is by all means a pleasure to meet you," he said as he extended his hand for that one opportunity to embrace hers.

"Great to meet you, Bishop Moore. Enjoy your evening and thanks for coming," Brayla said as she proceeded to walk away. Bishop excused himself and grabbed Brayla's attention. He extended his hand once again, hoping that this time, she'd accept.

Brayla smiled as she grabbed his hand and said, "Oh, I apologize. I wasn't trying to be rude by not shaking your hand."

The Scales of Love

"No problem...no problem at all," Bishop said in an eager, yet jittery tone.

"So what is it that you do, Bishop?" Brayla asked.

"I'm the Executive Director of IT at Tabor & Tabor."

As quickly as their conversation began it also ended. A soft voice called out Bishop's name, "Bishop! Bishop!" the mysterious woman yelled. "You ready?" she asked as she smiled, enclosing her arm into his.

Brayla smiled and looked to Bishop for a formal introduction of the woman.

As Bishop proceeded to make an introduction, a business partner and best friend of Bishop's named Ken intervened, "Great job man on that presentation today!"

As if Ken had just saved him from the most awkward moment of his life, Bishop exclaimed, "Thanks Ken!"

The woman nudged Bishop to head toward the door. Bishop offered his apologies to Brayla and asked to reconvene their conversation soon. Brayla offered her card and wished the couple a peaceful evening.

"I should have known then his intentions were no good," Brayla said to herself as she sat outside shaking her head. Looking down the street, she watched as Bishop's car vanished out of sight.

4

Rekindling the Flame

Sometimes if the flame goes out, it's better to leave it alone.

It was no secret that Bishop had fallen fast and hard for Brayla when they first met. To this day, he has always felt the same for her. Usher's, You Got it Bad had nothing on Bishop when it came to him pursuing Brayla. For the next two months, Brayla's office was filled with flowers, gifts and surprises from Bishop in his pursuit to win her back after their short breakup. His invitation for dinner was still on the table since Brayla refused to accept. However, through his persistency, he finally got Brayla to agree to dinner. She still questioned his motives.

Bishop, ecstatic that Brayla had finally accepted his dinner invitation, immediately made reservations at J Alexander's. "Great, I'll pick you up tonight at 7 p.m.," Bishop said.

Brayla responded, "That won't be necessary. I'll meet you there."

The Scales of Love

Bishop sounded a little discouraged and nervous, "Are you sure? I can pick you up. It's not an issue. After all, it is our first date in a while. Let me do the catering." Bishop insisted.

Brayla replied sternly, but in a soft tone, "I said no, and this is not a date. I'll meet you there at 7 p.m. and we'll see about the catering."

"Okay, 7 p.m. at J Alexander's. I'll meet you in the lobby," Bishop agreed.

Brayla rushed out of her office since she was late for lunch with the girls. "Wait till they find out I'm late because of dinner arrangements with Bishop. I'll never hear the end of it." Brayla arrived at Benihana just in time to see the girls being seated.

"Ladies," Brayla greeted them.

"It's about time," Sasha chimed in. "What took you so long? That's not like you not to be prompt."

"Well, I got a little detoured in my departure."

"Girl what are you talking about," Amerus asked.

"-Bishop!"

"What!?" the crew exclaimed in unison. "Bishop?!

So what's up with that?"

Barakah Miller

"Jewels, he has been on me like a strong safety going in for a tackle since our last brunch. Poppin' up at my house unannounced, calls, texts, and oh... need I mention all the flowers, gifts and surprises he conveniently sends to the office? We're having dinner tonight."

"Dinner!" Nia screamed as she looked awkwardly at Brayla. "Girl, I thought you weren't interested in rekindling that spark."

"I'm not, but no matter how I say no, he is so darn persistent. I figured we'll have dinner and I'll be up front with him again. He'll get it this time."

"I don't know, Bray," Sasha said. "I think you are treading on some dangerous flames. I know it's been over six months, but I know you. You truly love that man. Love like that don't vanish in no dang six months. All I'm saying is be careful, Bray. I know how you feel. I just don't want to see you get hurt. Remember, we are the cleanup crew."

"Girl, stop! I'll be alright. Thanks for caring so much but even though I have those feelings, I must admit I am a little concerned about losing my ground and giving into my emotions. He's so good at pushing the grain...dang."

"Are you sure you're up for this?" Amerus asked.

"Yes, I can handle Mr. Bishop Moore. I know him better than I like to admit."

The Scales of Love

"Well, do the dang thing," Amerus said.

"Girl, you so silly. Oh I gotta go! See you divas!"

"Enjoy yourself, but not too much," Nia said.

"Girl, I got this!"

A little after seven, Brayla arrives at J Alexander's. Before getting out of her car, she looks in the mirror and gives herself a pep talk.

"No matter what happens tonight, I will not let Bishop's charm move me to make emotional choices."

Bishop, standing in the lobby, looks out the window and sees Brayla walking up to the entrance. He opens the door for her as he smiles and gives her a kiss on the cheek. He inhales her fragrance and loses his train of thought momentarily as he is hypnotized.

The host escorts them to their table and Bishop proceeds to thank Brayla for accepting his invitation.

"I didn't think you would ever accept. Why are you being so hard, Bray? I mean, I know it's been a while, but I still feel the same about you. Just because we didn't see each other for all those months...my feelings for you never changed. My love for you remains the same...always!"

Brayla chuckled, "You're good, but not that good. Bishop, why are you so gong ho on getting me back? What, is there no marital bliss or is she having one of her so called mental episodes? Seriously, what's the catch? Because if you think I'm interested in playing any kind of 'role' or following your 'protocol,' I'm not the woman for that. Remembering your words Bishop...your word is all I had. If you cannot honor your word, you don't deserve to have me. The power of life and death lies within your own tongue."

"If that's how you really feel, you got it all wrong! Why can't you see things from my perspective? You know what I'm up against the stress, the work and my health. Look Brayla, why you gotta bring up old stuff?"

"Hold up! You were the one who said, "We both have to understand the situation and our 'role', whether we agree or disagree. We're not married or living together; therefore, we both know there are certain things that can't or won't be done. It's called 'protocol' since I can't use the word 'role.' As long as she's there, it is a 'role'. We're in it for each other. You take that anyway you feel love, but it's the truth. Period...Real talk!" Remember that Bishop? Those were your words only six months ago. Now you expect me to come running back into your arms? You must be losing it! My image of you can only be tainted by you and you've done a good job in proving yourself. Oh, let's not forget the gift you had for me...the one you said 'somebody' found and you gave it to your daughter."

Brayla tried to remain calm as that night replayed in her mind. Her heart started racing as she tried her hardest to fight back the tears. "Get it together," she coached herself. "You bet not let one tear drop in front of him." Brayla exhaled and took a drink of water before continuing. "At times, I'm just appalled by you."

"And as I said, those words weren't intended to hurt your feelings, Bray. I just spoke the truth. I mean dang, Bray. Why you being so hard on a man? What I got to do to show you my feelings for you are real? Brayla, I never said I stopped loving you."

"Unbelievable! How can you say you love me and your words were so harsh? It was as if you became a completely different person, like what we had was superficial and it meant nothing to you after all the time we've been together! What did I ever do to you for you to express those thoughts? It's apparent that those words were harboring in your heart; otherwise, you would have never spoken them." Brayla shook her head in disbelief of the memory. "Whose truth? Your truth?! Do you have any idea how you made me feel? Your words and actions have caused me so much unnecessary pain. For someone who's so persistent in professing their love for me, you sure have a peculiar way of showing and expressing it. How can I entertain the thought, Bishop? And if I did, how can I trust you with my heart? How can I trust that things will be different? After all, we're not married or living together."

"Cute, Brayla. Real cute," Bishops chuckled.

"What is it with you? How can you be so darn consistent in saying you love me when there has been no communication for months, just distance? I don't understand that! And on top of that, you're married!"

"Bray, why you always get upset? I give you what I can baby. My love doesn't change any less because I don't see you. Why is it so difficult for you to get that?! No strings attached, no games, and no mind playing. Bray, you're my heart. You'll always be my baby. Just because I don't love you the way you think I should doesn't mean I don't love you. For a person to go months without seeing you or communicating with you doesn't mean love has faded. For love to continue and remain the same, fresh from the moment that they met, simply means you have their heart. Bray, look at it this way. I'm in the service and deported off for a year or two. The separation doesn't change my love for you. It actually makes it stronger. You just gotta trust it, baby."

"But, Bishop you're..."

The Scales of Love

"No, Bray. Don't do that. I want you in my life regardless. The feeling I get from being with you, I never had before and I absolutely love it! You're my weakness, my kryptonite. We have something special. There's got to be a reason we keep trying at this on and off for six years, Bray. Come on, baby. For whatever reason, we can't seem to end."

"Wow! What'd you expect me to say?"

"Say that you'll take me back, that you still feel the same."

"Convince me to take you back. What are you offering?"

"Part ownership is what I'm offering, plus all the benefits that come with it. I want my spot back. I wanna be part of the team again. You know, the GM," Bishop smiled.

Brayla said sarcastically, "There's plenty of room on the bench with a lot of players with no playing time."

"Have you forgotten that I'm the GM? I own the team!" Bishop blurted out. They both burst out in laughter. "That's my girl. Loosen up," he said.

"Bishop, the fact that you had the audacity to speak those words to me and tell me about the gift... seriously... you could have played the gift part off. I appreciate the honesty; however, if you loved me as much as you continue to profess, there is no way possible you would have ever fixed your mouth to speak those words to me. Honestly, that's what was in your heart. Otherwise, you would have never said it. How can you expect me to entertain the thought of ever being with you after you chose to speak those words to me, of all people? That's not what our relationship was built up on. What happened to the mental part of our relationship, the intimacy? Did you forget that's how you got me in the first place? And what about Nyla? She is still there."

"Brayla, I know no matter what I say from this point on, I can't take back the past. I apologize for anything and everything that I may have done and said to hurt you or disappointment you. But Bray, I wouldn't be here right now at this moment if I didn't still love you and felt you didn't feel the same way. I know you do. Yes, I'm married. I know and this goes against the grain on every level. I know, so please stop throwing that in my face. Yes, Nyla is still my wife. It's not easy but at the same time, I have these feelings for you. I just can't seem to walk away and let you go. Maybe that's part of my problem. As hard as I've tried while we were apart to get over you, I just couldn't.

No matter how hard I try, at the end of the day, I had to take ownership of my feelings and admit to myself that I was still in love with you and that I wanted and needed you in my life, my world. But is that enough for you? I can't promise you that we're going to be together 24/7, but I can assure you that my love for you will never change, regardless. Baby, I love you regardless, no matter what. Why can't you see that? Why can't you enjoy the times we are together instead of harping on all that other nonsense?"

"Bishop, this is more than what I anticipated from you. I don't know if I'm strong enough to be with you under those circumstances. And I don't know if I'll ever be able to communicate how I really feel. I'm not comfortable telling you." In an instance Brayla thinks about her father and Symone and wants to be transparent with Bishop, however she knows the timing is not right.

"Baby, don't be afraid of what you feel," Bishops insisted. You excite every part of me, Bray...deep within to the depths of my soul. I've never had these feelings before for any other woman not even her. It's different with you. You're the only woman who's ever made me feel this way. Baby, I don't wanna feel this way all by myself. I know you feel it, too. Brayla, why are you fighting what we both know? I know it's not right. But I can't help what I'm feeling for you. My feelings for you are real. Brayla, why are you looking away? You can't look me in my eyes and tell me you're still in love with me, too?"

"Bishop, if you feel as strongly as you say you do about me, why are you still married to Nyla? Oh wait...it's not that easy right?! Thanks for dinner. I think I should leave now."

"Wait, you just gon' walk out on me? Okay, I'm sorry. I just want you to understand how I feel. Don't let me expressing myself send you off. Can we finish our dinner and work on rebuilding our friendship? I don't want you to leave, especially not like this."

"Alright, I like you too...as a friend," Brayla asserted as she sat back down.

5

I Got This!

It's hard to tell the mind to stop loving someone if the heart still does.

Brayla arrived home after her evening with Bishop. She checked on her babies and then crawled up onto her chaise to relax and reflect on the evening and all that Bishop said.

"Whoa, this is way too much to digest in one evening. God, I love this man but I can't tell him I feel the same way. I wasn't expecting all that information from him. Lord, what am I gonna do?"

Brayla closed her eyes to meditate but the phone rang before she could begin. It was Bishop. "Lord, what now. Hello?"

"Hey baby, just calling to make sure you made it home okay."

"Thanks Bishop, that was very thoughtful of you. I'm sure that's not the only reason you called," Brayla said in a suggestive tone.

The Scales of Love

"You know me all too well," Bishop bellowed. "Since you brought it up, I was hoping you would join me for a night cap or just an evening stroll. I can come to you and we can walk around your neighborhood or up to the park. What do you say?" Bishop wishfully proposed.

Brayla shook her head in disbelief, as if he could see her. "Amazing. What else could you possibly have to say? I think you said more than enough tonight."

Bishop chimed in, "Baby, I just want to see you one last time this evening, if it's okay with you."

"Bishop, I don't think that's a good idea. Besides..."

Bishop cut her off, "–Bray, come on! It's me!"

Brayla interrupted, "I know, that's the problem!"

"What's that supposed to mean?"

"Where are you? I'm sure you're close in vicinity."

"As a matter of fact, I'm about five minutes from you. Is that my yes?" Bishop asked with excitement in his voice.

"Come on man. I'll meet you in front of my house."

Brayla changed her shoes and grabbed a jacket before heading downstairs to greet Bishop. Bishop pulled up as Brayla walked toward the sidewalk. Bishop got out of his

SUV, walked up to Brayla with his hand extended and said, "Shall we?"

Brayla looked at him suspiciously. She grabbed his hand and they proceeded with their evening walk while holding hands.

"I miss this," Bishop said.

"Miss what?"

"You and I. The stillness of the quietness where it's only the two of us and our hearts share the same heartbeat. Remember that? How I used to hold you after we made love and the rhythm of our heartbeats would always be in unison? The joy you always brought to my heart and the smile you gave me the moment I looked at you."

"Bishop look. Yes, I love you and care about you, and I always will. I just don't believe my heart could take another separation or anymore disappointments from you. Period! I'm not built for this and this is not right. My heart belongs to you, and I have been trying really hard to move forward and get you completely out my system. There is so much more for me to experience, but I can't if you still have my heart. And you're not making it any easier at this moment."

"Bray, I completely understand if it's not enough for you and you want out. But I know you love me and I love you. I would hope it was enough, but can you honestly say you

The Scales of Love

can accept us not being a part of each other's lives? It's when you say things like that, that I wonder also if it's enough, regardless how I tell you I feel."

"How can you expect it to be enough?! Don't you get it? I love you, and it's real and it scares me. I can't be a temporary emotion or fix for you and I won't be. Don't you get it? This love that I have for you can't and won't settle to be just a piece of your life. All or nothing. You know that Bishop."

"Why does it have to be all or nothing? I'm trying Bray, help me out. I understand how you feel and I won't force it. I just need you to know my feelings toward you are real, always have been."

As Brayla prepared to say, "No, it's not enough," images of Symone flashed through her mind and a tear drop rolled down her face as she thought of the situation.

"Bishop, it's not just about us. There's so much more at stake. Have you considered that our actions not only affect us, but the people around us that we love and care about dearly as well?"

"Yes, I have," Bishops replied.

"What about your life taking up too much of you to make anyone else happy but what's around you?"

"Bray, again, I can't change what I've done or said in the past. Baby, all I can do is continue to tell you how I feel as you do the same. You do deserve more, and maybe I'm not the man to give you that. I don't know what the future holds. But I do know what I feel for you is real and all I can do is try my best to be the best me I can for you."

There's a moment of silence as Bishop moved in to kiss Brayla. They kiss and join hands as they head back to Brayla's house. Bishop walked Brayla to the door and leaned in for another kiss as he said, "Thank you. Good night!"

Bishop arrived home after his evening with Brayla shortly after 2 a.m. Nyla was still up working in the home office as she heard Bishop come through the garage. Bishop walked in and noticed the light on as Nyla greeted him in the living room.

"Hey babe. It's late, why are you still up?"

"Working...where have you been?"

"Out with some friends," Bishop replied as he leaned in and embraced Nyla, smiling.

"On a weekday? That's not like you baby."

The Scales of Love

"I know, but I'm here now. How was your day? I missed you with all the traveling I've been doing. We don't see each other much lately."

"I agree love. My day has been busy, as usual. The kids, work and going over these manuals. Whew, it's more than enough to keep anybody busy. Why don't we go upstairs and enjoy each other while we have the opportunity?"

"I'd like that," Bishop replied.

6

Following Your Heart

Go where your heart takes you.

Brayla walked upstairs to check on DJ and then proceeded to Symone's room. She opened her door and stood there while watching Symone sleep. She walked in and lied next to her. As she embraced Symone, tears rolled down her face. Brayla closed her eyes and said a quiet prayer before Symone woke up.

"Mommy, you're crying. What's wrong, mama?"

Brayla startled, replied, "Baby, God has just blessed me with the most beautiful angel and I'm so grateful to Him that He has given you to me. That's all, baby. Go back to sleep."

Symone smiled and gave Brayla a kiss and closed her eyes. They cuddled in the moonlight-lit bedroom.

The next morning, Brayla and Symone were awakened by the aroma of an early morning breakfast. They looked at each other and smiled.

The Scales of Love

Symone said, "Bruh bruh is cooking, mommy!" Symone jumped up and ran downstairs into the arms of DJ. "Good morning, Big Brother!" Symone shouted.

"Good morning, Princess!"

Brayla walked in and said, "What is all this for?"

"Just showing my appreciation, mom. That's all!"

The phone rang as Symone darted to answer it. "Good morning! Mommy, it's Auntie Nia!"

Brayla took the phone from Symone. "Hey Nia, why the early morning call?" Skeptical, Brayla knew it was about dinner with Bishop.

Nia replied, "Girl, you already know. What happened last night with you and Bishop? No details needed. I just want to make sure you're good about whatever decision you went with."

Brayla went into the living room as she tells Nia that she went with her heart.

"Which was?" Nia asked.

"I gave in. I know it's wrong but at the last moment, I gave in. It had nothing to do with me. It's complicated, as if it couldn't get any more complicated. Nia, we've been through so much together and so much is at stake. I did what I thought was best at that moment. My decision had nothing to do with me."

"Then who, Bray? Who?"

"I can't say at the moment. But he still does have my heart. Sasha was right. Love like that doesn't just go away in six months. I do believe he is sincere but at the same time, I am afraid. It's a risk I have to take. If it doesn't work out, I will end it. But I have to give myself the opportunity to reveal some things to Bishop. It's gonna take a while, but I'll get to it."

"Well, how are you both going to make it work? You know you both are workaholics and you know how you get when you don't get his time. That was part of your dilemma last time, Bray! Girl, I just pray God gives you the wisdom you need as you proceed with this relationship. Let's pray. Father God, I just pray that you will give the wisdom Brayla needs from you at this hour. Only you know Father what it is she is dealing with. Give her the comfort, strength and discernment she needs. Protect her heart and her family. Let no hurt, harm or danger come near their dwelling. Shield her but be her help as she moves forward in her decision. Only you can give her the wisdom and peace she is seeking in this relationship. Father, we thank you for all you are doing right now, in Jesus' name, Amen!"

"Love you girl. I so needed that!" Brayla said, wiping tears from her eyes.

The Scales of Love

"Bray, just be careful and remember there is a cost that comes with this."

"Yeah I know. Believe me, I know!"

"We'll hook up later," Nia said.

"Okay, later."

Brayla's cell phone chimed again but this time, it was Bishop. "Three text messages and it's not even 9:30 yet."

"Good morning luv! How's your morning?"

"Can't wait to see you again! I enjoyed you last night."

"Hey cutie, let's do lunch later."

"Wow!" Brayla bellowed. "He is sounding like a man who's in love."

Brayla decided to respond back.

"I would love to Papi!"

Bishop chimed right back, "You just made my day! I'll pick you up at 2 p.m."

"I'll be waiting love."

DJ walked into the living room and said, "So you and Bishop are an item again?"

"Excuse me?"

"Mom ..."

"I heard what you said DJ; it's the way you said it! Why are you asking me that and where did that come from?"

"I saw him pull up the other day when I took Symone to the park."

"Oh, I see. For the moment, I guess you can say that."

"Mom, are you going to tell him this time?"

"Tell him what, DJ?" Brayla asked, frustrated that she even had to have this conversation with a child.

"Mom, come on. Symone!"

"Quiet it down! I don't want your sister to hear this conversation. I've been thinking about that. Honestly baby, that's the only reason I even considered talking to him again. But that's something I have to do in my own time and it doesn't concern you. Thanks for being so protective," Brayla said with a gentle smile.

"Well, mom. The sooner you tell him the truth, the better you'll feel and you can move on with your life without him. You deserve so much better!"

"You're right. In time...now go get your sister ready for today."

The Scales of Love

Brayla stepped into her home office to try to get some work done, but fell into a flashback of Bishop and her first separation. Things had been up and down with Brayla and Bishop over the course of four months. Brayla was frustrated and all too familiar with Bishop's actions. Brayla recalled one particular phone call.

"Hello, Love!"

"Bishop?! Why does it seem like ever since your surgery, you seem to be distancing yourself? What's happening to us?" Brayla cried as she waited for his response.

"I've just had a lot on my mind. Nothing personal towards you. I'm laid up here on my butt with people waiting on me. I'm not accustomed to this. I need to be out taking care of things, not laying up here on my behind."

"Why are you shutting me out? You know I'm here for you. Don't do that to me."

"Baby, I love you and I want more than anything to be up under you. But I gotta get me right before I can even step to you properly. What you gone do with a cripple man?" Bishop chuckled. "I need you to be strong for the both of us."

"You know I got you, boo. Just don't leave me hanging in the dark."

"I won't. I promise. I'm sorry Brayla, I'll do better."

Another three weeks went by and once again, Brayla was disappointed because Bishop didn't keep his promise. Finally fed up, she texted Bishop.

"I'm shutting you out of my life, out of my heart, out of my thoughts and my memories! I don't want to know you anymore. Erase my numbers and pics."

"Wow! If that's what you really feel, what can I really say to convince you otherwise? I don't know what else to say," he replied.

"You never seem to know what to say. Maybe that's how I ended up here instead of always trying to say something. DO sumthin!"

"Sorry I couldn't be what you need at this moment in my life. I think that you're forever beautiful. And you will forever remain close to my heart. My life right now, you would never understand. Thank you for always trying to be my sunshine."

That was the first of many separations between Brayla and Bishop. One month later, they were together again and for the first time, they were intimate. That changed the course of their relationship. Bishop became distant all of a sudden and Brayla was confused with the mixed signals he was sending her.

The Scales of Love

"Bishop, why does it seem as if you're intentionally distancing yourself from me? I thought we were just beginning again and this was not just one-sided. What's going on with you?"

"I still think the world of you, Brayla. But after that day, I felt convicted. And it's been on my mind so much. I've constantly had headaches, something I've never have. It's nothing you did wrong. It's all me!"

"So, are you saying it's over? You said that you were never going anywhere and that we would always have each other; that we were building upon our relationship."

"Our bond has always been strong. Even though I feel conviction, I feel in my heart you are a one-of-a-kind special person. I wish I knew what the future holds. Then, I would have some answers. But I don't know, baby. I'm just taking it one day at a time. Don't want to hurt anyone. I just want to make sure what it is God wants me to do."

Devastated, Brayla said, "I understand."

Seven months later, Bishop texted Brayla out of the blue.

"I was in the hospital again. I had emergency surgery on Monday. I have a fractured jaw. I have a metal plate holding and aligning my jaw and teeth back in their proper place. I can barely talk and I can't eat anything solid for six weeks.

I'm still in so much pain. Sorry that you feel like I haven't talked to you on purpose. I wish I could now."

"After all this time – sorry to hear. Hope all is well with you soon. But you're the last person I expected to hear from. That message was sent weeks ago."

"Where is this all coming from? I was just letting you know I was in the hospital and it turned into all this. Dang! I thought we were always good. What do you want?"

"What do I want?! You pursued me, made me fall in love with you, then you distance yourself because you can't decide what you want and then you have the audacity to assume 'we good' and now you're asking me, what I want? Where do we stand? I mean out of the blue, you just wanted me to know you're in the hospital? Why? What's the point? We haven't spoken in months and you needed me to know this?"

"I don't know. Why are you asking me this now? We haven't been talkin' or anything. How am I supposed to feel...really?"

"Ummm...you reached out to me!"

"I guess we can only be close friends. If we want more, we both know the complications that come with that."

"I thought you said we were done with that, especially after that day."

The Scales of Love

"I did but it had nothing to do with that day. I just had to do some self-evaluating. I enjoyed everything about that day. I still think the world of you. You don't love me no more, huh?"

Brayla sat up in her chaise, shaking her head. "Why did I put myself right back in the fire? After all that, could it possibly get any better than that? Bishop's intentions are good, they just don't always go in my favor. I know he means well, but I really can't put myself through this. Hopefully with time, things have changed and things will be different this time. Following my heart is going to get me in a lot of trouble!"

7

A Love Jones

When love strikes, pay attention!

Over the next two months, Bishop was on his P's & Q's. Brayla was amazed at his efforts. It was as if she had fallen in love all over again with a new man! Every opportunity they had, they were together. They met for breakfast, lunch and dinner. The flowers, gifts and surprises continued as if Brayla became Bishop's one and only lady. Brayla even started to allow him over to her house. DJ was shocked that Bishop passed the test to make it through the front door, something he thought he would never see. DJ loved his mother and was very protective of her. Bishop picked up on that after reacquainting with DJ. He understood DJ's demeanor and assured him that he had his mother's best interest at heart.

When Bishop saw Symone, he was shocked to see how much she had grown in the last eight months. "Wow! Symone is just growing into a beautiful young lady like her mama," Bishop said, smiling. As DJ and Brayla made eye

The Scales of Love

contact, Brayla motioned for DJ to take Symone outside to play.

"Bray, you are doing a fabulous job with the kids. And DJ, he is quite the gentleman. Protective of his mother, no doubt," Bishop snickered.

"And you, Mr. Moore," Brayla said, "I must say you have a way with children yourself. You too are an awesome father, if nothing else," Brayla joked. "Seriously, Bishop. You are a great father. Your children are blessed to have you as their daddy. I must admit that is one of the qualities I just love about you Bishop."

"Thanks baby," Bishop smiled and reached for Brayla, pulling her near to embrace her. "I love you so much," Bishop professed. You have no idea what you mean to me, all we've been through. I feel like I can trust you with my life. You know you have my heart always," Bishop said in the most sincere voice.

Brayla cringed as she thought of what his reaction would be the moment she told him that Symone is his daughter. "Are you sure about that," Brayla asked in an unsure tone.

"No doubt," Bishop replied. "Why do you sound so surprised?

"It's just that you seem different than the last few times we were together. I see the change in you. I'm just wondering how long before you revert back to the Bishop I've come to know. I don't mean that in a bad way. This is good, just a little questionable."

"Babe, why are you saying this?"

"It's just when things seem too good to be true, they usually are. That's all. Take that how you will. I know that you love me and whatever happens, you will love me regardless. I just wonder how far you really mean that, that's all. When things are good, they're good. But the moment things go left, you get in your 'be by myself mode' and shut me out. I hate when you do that."

"Girl, don't worry your pretty self with all that unnecessary drama. You know I ain't going nowhere! You got me, baby. Let's just enjoy each other. I ain't going nowhere. You just better hold on to your baby!"

"I got you, Big Daddy! Why you say that, boo?"

"You got my heart," Bishop replied, looking Brayla in her eyes. After a moment of silence, Bishop caressed Brayla's cheek and told her, "You had me from the moment I saw you. I just had to figure out how I was gonna balance us and my situation. I couldn't at first. That's why we had so many separations."

The Scales of Love

"So you're saying no matter what happens between us, you're always gonna be present in my life, huh?"

"What could possibly go wrong, Bray? I'm happy, you're happy. Baby, stop with the calamitous talk. There's nothing you could do or say to cause me to leave you. What, you trying to push me away already?" Bishop asked, jokingly.

"Of course not! Let's go out on the patio. I wanna watch Symone as she plays."

"No problem." Brayla grabbed Bishop's hand and led him to the back patio where they had tea and continued sharing conversation. DJ left and went to the park to shoot hoops with his boys.

"So Bishop, how's the family?"

"Great! Everybody's just growing up so fast. You know Kyndel is a sophomore in college now."

"What!" Brayla exclaimed. "Wow, time sure does go by fast."

"And Ayanna is a senior in high school. The twins, BJ and CJ are freshman in high school."

"And the other half?" Brayla gestured with a smile.

"She's well," Bishop replied.

"What about yaya and papa? What are they up to?"

"Retirement! They are the coolest. I'll let them know you asked about them."

"No doubt," Brayla smiled. "No wonder you have so much free time on your hands. Your nest is pretty much independent. That must be a relief for you. No more chaperoning, playing taxi cab and all the other duties that come with teenagers."

"Well, somewhat. The boys are in just about every sport you could think of and Ayanna is the music and dance queen. They are all into something. Kyndel is in Ohio so she comes home on the weekends sometimes if she's not working or training. You know, it all works out."

"But..." Brayla said.

"But what?"

"You and Nyla?"

"We cool."

"So, you saying she don't be trippin' with all your unaccounted time away from the nest?"

"I run it," Bishop responded quickly.

"Yeah right!" Brayla cut him off. "Boy please! You know she got you on a leash. She still be up in your phone sending messages to people she don't know to stay away from her man?!" Brayla chuckled as Bishop replied, "You're not funny."

"Well you were the one who told me that mess, so don't get mad at me. I believe that just as much as you want me to believe she's crazy!"

"Fair enough," Bishop replied. "Can we change the subject?"

"Be my guest," Brayla laughed.

"You know Bray, we haven't spent one night together since we've revived our relationship."

"So what's your point?" Brayla asked.

Bishop grabbed Brayla's hands and caressed them as he looked in her eyes. "I want to make passionate love to you like we always used to do. I miss being able to hold your body naked next to mine. Even if we don't make love, I just want to lay naked next to you and feel your body close to mine."

"Oh...um, I don't think I'm ready for that quite yet."

"Why is that, Bray?"

"I just want us to move slow, very slow. I need to know we're gonna last past another six months. I can't give of myself to you like that anymore not knowing if you're here today and gone tomorrow."

"Bray, I'm not going anywhere baby! Haven't you been listening to anything I've said? It's me, Bray. Tell me, what are you really afraid of?"

"You disappointing me again, the distance and lack of communication...you know the routine of we on this week, off two weeks. Back on three weeks, off again next week."

"Baby that was my work schedule. I have no control over that. You know you got a working man 24/7. My job is very demanding and so is yours. Woman, you balancing three businesses and you don't hear me complaining."

"Well tell that to my heart."

"Bray, you know how I felt when I was off and money was tight. I was out there tryna make up for it. It had nothing to do with you or us. Baby, don't take that personal. I know life sometimes gets the best of us, but I'm here now."

"I know, Bishop. It's just you know I love being under you when we have time like this and you have set the tone for it. I've grown accustomed to it, so I expect it. When there is distance, I feel like you're stepping away from me. Honestly, if you can't continue what you started, you shouldn't be so eager to pick it back up."

"Bray, girl you've got it all wrong. I would never step away from you unless you pushed me away. I'm not going nowhere. Just don't push me away baby. As far as the distance, my love for you doesn't change just because I don't see you, even though life sometimes gets in the way. Babe, I need you to get that! Real talk!"

"Got it," Brayla said, leaning in to kiss Bishop. Brayla caressed his face and said, "Thank you. I apologize for allowing my emotions from the past and past relationships to shatter my faith in you. I love you and I'm so in love with you Mr. Bishop Moore!"

Bishop leaned in and passionately kissed Brayla before replying, "I love you too, and I couldn't be more happy and in love than this moment right now."

They both smiled and Brayla told Bishop, "I'll reconsider your request."

Bishop anxiously replied, "We can do the dang thing now! I want you so bad, baby! You have no idea. I'm at your mercy!"

"Oooh wee, Big Daddy! Come here!"

They stepped inside the dining room behind the curtain so Symone was still visible by sight, but couldn't see them. Bishop caressed Brayla's body and they kissed passionately. Bishop softly spoke, "I want your lips to taste my body, all of me, baby."

Brayla replied, "You're giving me chills. I want you, too. Whew, I can't wait! I'm ready now for you. Call me soon!"

"Okay," Bishop replied, heading for the door. "I hate I have to leave, dang but I gotta get to work. It's gonna be a long, horny night for Bishop." He smiled as he walked out the side door.

Brayla headed back to the patio as her phone rang. It was Nia.

"Hey lady, what's going on with you?"

"Bray, just calling to see how you're doing."

"Girl, I'm great! How's the fam?"

"We're good. Don't get me wrong, I trust you and know you can handle your situation. I'm just concerned about you getting in too deep and finding yourself in a love hangover."

"Nia! I'm well. Believe me, I know myself and Bishop far too well for that to ever happen again."

"Girl all I'm saying is pay attention and when you find yourself questioning his silence, put all the clues on the table and tell yourself what you see. Girl, you give great advice. Start applying your own advice to your own situation. I know Bishop loves you, despite his situation. However, woman to woman, he is a man and he wants what he wants, regardless of his vows. He wants her cake and yours. He's selfish and self-serving. Hopefully, you will eventually see that. I'm praying for you and that God gives you clarity and reveals Bishop's heart and motives to you."

"Thanks for caring and keeping it real. I love how you go raw on a sistah. I hear what you're saying but I made a choice and at the moment, I'm not ready to reconsider my options. I love him so and I just can't get myself past that. I know this is not right and I'm starting to wonder myself if it is worth it. But I have other things to consider as well. I don't know why or how I will but through prayer, God will help me."

"Bray, trust what you feel but know you are very attractive. Any man would be honored to have you. We'll chat again soon. I'll be in touch."

"Thanks love, see you soon."

8

High Off Love

After the honeymoon, the buzz goes away.

Brayla found herself in a daze, thinking about the latest evening of festivities with Bishop. "Man, I want my baby to make love to me like we used to! Ugh, I can feel him inside me now. What have I done? Once again, I'm high off Mr. Moore!"

Her phone chimed. When she picked it up, she noticed it was a message from Bishop and she instantly opened it. "I love you so much. I would like nothing more than to be up under you, giving you all the loving you need. Tell me what you want me to do?"

Brayla smiled and responded, "You know my passion for you. I want to be wrapped up in your arms, embracing your strength and love, as you gently caress my body with your kisses...making love to my mind..."

Brayla laid her phone down as memories flashed through her mind of her relationship with Bishop. She thought to herself, "We have had some fond memories,

The Scales of Love

good and bad." But the one memory that flashed through her mind at that moment was their breakup, from the first time they made love and how he came, conquered and took what he wanted and was out. Brayla felt a tugging in her stomach as she recalled that moment. Hurt and confused, she reflected on that conversation.

"You still didn't answer my previous question. Do you or have you ever really listened to me? I feel that you haven't and I've let a lot of things go unsaid, mostly because you made me feel, just like now, that you didn't want to hear it. I feel like you took what you wanted and was out, and now you try to pacify me. You only needed me when it was convenient for you."

"That's not how it is at all. I stay away 'cause I don't want to hurt you. You just can't see that! I want you in my life always. I thought I could handle us and my situation. I couldn't 'cause my heart was real toward you. Now you're saying I got what I wanted? Wow! I wish that day would have never happened, then you wouldn't feel that way about me. That is so far from the truth, baby."

"Wow! You make me feel like I'm in this all by myself and it doesn't bother you that I feel this way."

"I'm saying I love you no matter what! Even though life sometimes gets in the way, it's not like you're here every day. You don't call me every day, so why do you make it seem as if it's all on me?"

Barakah Miller

"I love you, too! I don't call you because I don't want to feel rejected and when I did in the past, you don't answer! Besides you the man, you suppose to be calling me not expecting me to ride you. So if I want to be with you, I got to come to and call you?! Guess we have different views on us and what a relationship consist of."

"That's not what I said! It seems like you're trying to argue for no reason. I'm not in the mood to do this so..."

"I'm not trying to argue with you! Why do you always say that, as if it's a scapegoat for you to avoid the situation at hand? Whatever Bishop!"

Her phone rang, bringing her back into reality from her flashback. It's Nia, again,

"Hello."

"Hey, Bray. How are things going? Just wanted to check up on you."

"Thanks, girl. I'm well and Bishop is really trying hard to stay at the forefront of my thoughts. It's as if he's a different man. I love it, but I'm also wondering if I'm going to push him away before I get a chance to open my heart completely up."

"Bray, if you love him like I know you do, don't keep him guessing. Don't force him to read between the lines. Just come out and say what's in your heart. He can only have respect for you being completely honest with him. Listen, when I divorced my ex, it was hard at first thinking about all we've been through. But, at the end of the day, I had to do what I needed to for the kids and, most importantly, me! I refused to stay in an environment that was unconducive to my growing and happiness."

"I get that, Nia. It's just that at times, I'm afraid."

"Afraid of what?! Baby, there is no need to be afraid of what you feel. If he loves you, and I'm positive he does, despite his situation, unfortunately. His response is not going to be as bad as you may think it will be. After all the cheating, the lies, betrayal from my ex girl, me being completely honest with myself about him and us is where I got the strength to move forward and put all that behind me. Then God blessed me with putting James back in my life. Being married to an NFL player or any professional athlete is not all it's cracked up to be. Trust me. People want to glamourize the life of a professional athlete and being married to one as if it's the ideal life. Honey, it's so far from that. Being in the spotlight doesn't make it any easier. At any given moment, you are probed by the media and your peers. They are human just like everybody else with imperfections. As with any relationship, it takes work from both parties. It's not gonna be no Mrs. Leave it to Beaver type of situation. Marriage in itself is W-O-R-K and the test comes from staying together in spite of your differences. At the end of the day, it's not about the wedding or the honeymoon; it's about making it work, growing, staying together and keeping God as the pilot. The three-cord theory--you, him and God. Once we choose to remove God from our relationship, we give the devil free range to test us on every level."

"I'm learning that, Nia. And God is tugging at my heart; He is so patient with me. I know what I should do, but I just need time to get that to settle in my mind. Guess I'm not as strong as you say I am. I'm not fully ready to give up on Bishop or us."

"Bray, you are one of the strongest, giving, loving women I know. Don't let love deceive you. If God ain't in it, question it, is all I'm saying. You deserve a man who gets that and is willing to love you for you and give you all of him, totally and completely. I hate to say it, but Bishop just may not be that man. Nothing personal. Look, sometimes who you love can't take you to the levels God is trying to get you to. So we have to choose if we gone flow with God's plan or stay in bondage in a relationship that will eventually break us down."

"Wisdom of pearls from one of God's most precious jewels! Love you, girl. I appreciate the talk and wisdom. I guess this is the part where I ask myself are my wants in alignment with my worth? I'll get there in time. I know I will. We'll talk soon. I got to get to this contract sitting here on my desk."

The Scales of Love

"Love you, Bray, and ease up a little. Don't lose yourself trying to accommodate a relationship that doesn't have your best interest at heart. Be good to you. See ya!"

A knock at her office door distracted her thoughts.

"Excuse me, Ms. Thompson. There's a Mr. Moore here to see you. Should I escort him in?" her assistant asked.

"Sure, thank you, Olivia."

"Good afternoon, beautiful!" Bishop smiled as he greeted Brayla with a kiss and purple roses.

"Aw, babe! Thank you. You remembered! Impressive! One point for Bishop."

"Girl, I see I have to keep reminding you ain't nothing but layups and three pointers coming from the MVP now GM. I own the team remember?!"

"You sold on that, huh?" Brayla laughed as she set her roses by the window in her office. "Since that's what you really want, I know I have part ownership plus all the benefits that come with it, Daddy!"

"Fo sho, I wouldn't have it any other way. You know you're my love. Bray, you got my heart woman. Ain't no escaping that!" Bishop smiled and winked at Brayla.

"You're too much, babe," Brayla smiled, gesturing for Bishop to have a seat.

"I will if you join me."

"Of course I will," Brayla said, smiling.

"No, I mean here." Bishop grabbed Brayla's hand and twirled her to sit on his lap.

"Bishop! I can't sit on your lap. I'm at work and my door is wide open in case you're blind!"

"Close it..."

"You're a naughty boy."

"I can show you better than I can tell you, Ms. Thompson."

Brayla closed her office door as Bishop walked up behind her and gently put his arms around her. "There's nothing wrong with love in the middle of the afternoon," Bishop whispered in Brayla's ear. "Make love to me...now." Bishop groaned softly to Brayla as he removed Brayla's jacket.

Brayla said, "I remember you were always the first one naked. Now you want to undress me."

"Bishop said, "I want to enjoy you today...all of you! Let me cater to you," Bishop whispered to Brayla.

"As tempting as that sounds, and my body is screaming, 'Go ahead, Daddy, take care of Mama,' we can't."

"Bray, what's wrong?"

"Nothing. I've enjoyed every moment we've shared since we got back together. I just have a lot on my mind, that's all. I think we need to wait. I'm not sure where this is all going and before I give myself to you again, I have to know 'we' are going to get past some things we need to work on. I know you can agree on that."

"Maybe you're right. I have been trying to figure out what it is between us that keeps bringing us back together over and over again. One thing that is for sure and has never changed is my love for you. I miss holding you, being under you…you are my peace. I'm in a different place when I'm with you and I hate having to leave from under it. You are so good to me. At times, I think to myself that I don't deserve you."

"You're right…you don't!" Brayla smiled, before continuing. "How could something so good be so wrong? I mean, what we've always had was good. Our chemistry is unbelievable. Nothing comes close to what I've shared with you B."

"I know what you mean, Bray. It's as if we were made for each other – just bad timing, circumstances and life in general. I hate things have to be this way between us, which leads me to this. I have to go away on company business for at least a week or two. Don't trip please. Don't ruin the atmosphere."

"Where?" Brayla asked.

"Out of the country," Bishop responded.

"Mhm," Brayla replied.

"Bray, don't do this. I know what you're thinking and it's not like that."

"Oh, so you think you can still read my thoughts before I speak them?" Brayla gestured for Bishop to move out of her way as she walked toward her desk.

"I knew you would respond this way. That's why I was hesitant to tell you."

"No, don't be. I'm glad you did. I trust you. I understand. Work right?" Brayla asked with a long sigh.

Bishop sighed, "Come here, Bray. Look baby, this doesn't mean things are going to drastically change between us. I'll only be gone two weeks at the max."

"One thing for sure about being wifey, you always know that no matter where he travels, he'll always be coming home."

"What's that supposed to mean?!" Bishops asked in an irritated voice. "See there you go jacking up the mood. You're my baby! Why can't we just enjoy each other? No drama, no emotional rollercoaster episodes. Just you and me in the moment, cherishing one another. Why is that so difficult for you when you know what I'm always up against? Dang, baby!"

"Alright, I apologize," Brayla said. "It's just work always seem to be your MO for not communicating with me."

"Baby, you're a business woman. You of all people should understand my work schedule and ethic. I'm sorry for being so busy all the time. Life and work does sometime get in the way. You gotta understand that." Bishop paused, before continuing, "You got a life with responsibilities outside of you and I, and so do I. You have to always get upset. I give you what I can give, baby. My love doesn't change any less because I don't see you. We're not always going to agree but baby, let's agree to disagree without losing sight of the love we have for each other. Look how far we've come babe?!"

"You're absolutely correct. When you put it like that, how can I not agree with you B?"

"Girl, you gotta trust me. What happened to the faith you always had for us...for me?" Bishop asked, reminding Brayla of her former commitment.

"I think you should leave now," Brayla insisted. "I have a presentation in 20 minutes."

"Oh, so you puttin' me out now?" Bishop joked.

"Yes, I am!" Brayla said with a straight face.

9

The Balancing Act

Balance is not allowing anyone to love you any less than you love yourself. - Excerpt from 'Eat, Pray, Love'

Brayla told Olivia to clear her calendar for the rest of day and that after her presentation, she would be available via her cell phone. As Brayla is giving her presentation, Olivia buzzed the conference room to inform her that a package had been delivered for her.

Brayla finished her presentation and called Nia, Sasha and Amerus on a conference call.

"Hey, jewels!"

"What? I can't believe we hearing from you, Ms. High Off Love," Sasha joked.

"Good hearing your voice as well Sash," Brayla said. "The reason why I called is because we are so overdue for a girl time cocktail. Let's meet up tonight," Brayla suggested.

"I'm in," Amerus chimed in. "I miss my divas!"

The Scales of Love

Nia said, "Let me check with my boo and I'll give you a call back. Ok girls..."

"Mrs. Sasha, are you in or out?" Amerus asked.

"Definitely count me in!"

"Let's meet up at The Poetry Pit about 7ish. See you dolls then."

Brayla rushed home to spend some time with her babies before heading out with the girls. DJ and Symone came in the kitchen to assist Brayla with dinner.

"So how was your day, mama?" Symone asked.

"It just got better, smooches," Brayla said as she kissed Symone's cheek.

"Thanks mommy! Can I set the table?"

"You sure can, angel."

"So what's poppin' with DJ?"

"Nothing much, just thinking about which scholarship I 'ma take. I really love Michigan, but I kinda wanna go out of state so I'm weighing Iowa."

"Both are great teams in the Big 10! I'm sure you'll make the best decision for you."

"Mom, I was kinda hoping you would put a little of your persuasion in on it."

"Baby, I can't make that decision for you. At the end of the day, it's about what you want and what you think is best for DJ. Don't get me wrong; I too want the best for you. But you're a young man now and you're gonna have to make that decision on your own. Besides, you know I'm biased to Michigan. So I don't know why you would even ask me that." They both laughed. "Come here and give your mama a hug. I love you. You know that, right?"

"Yes ma'am. I love you too, mom. Thanks for always having our backs and sacrificing so much for us. I know you've only done the best you could with what you had and what you knew how. I love you for that. You my girl," DJ said joyfully, smiling.

"Thanks babe. Now wash your hands and mix up that salad," Brayla instructed.

"I got you," DJ smiled.

Symone ran into the kitchen. "Mommy, I finished setting the table. Can I help with anything else please?"

"Let's see," Brayla thought for a moment. "Aha, can you put the tea and lemonade on the table in the center, or is it too heavy for you?"

"I got it," Symone said cheerfully.

"Okay, make sure you use your muscles and both hands."

"I will."

"So mom, how was your day at the office?" DJ asked.

"It was refreshing, yet productive. I gave my presentation today to that company that wants to partner with one of our companies."

"How did that go?"

"I think it went well. Here, help me set the table with dinner. I gotta meet the girls later."

"Girls gone wild night, huh?" DJ joked.

"Boy, come on in here," Brayla nudged him.

Symone walked in the dining room with the package that was delivered to Brayla during her presentation. "Mommy, what's this?"

"Oh, just a little something from Mr. Moore, I assume."

"Aren't you going to open it?" Symone asked.

"Not right now. Go put it back where you found it."

"Yes, ma'am."

"Oh so, Mr. Do Right Now, I mean Bishop," DJ joked, "got a little chivalry going on. Just when I thought I had underestimated him."

"DJ, stop it!" Brayla said sternly.

"Mom, I'm not saying I dislike the dude. I'm just saying considering the truth of the matter..."

Brayla cut him off and immediately told DJ to stay in his place.

"Yes, ma'am," DJ said, hanging his head. "Sorry mom!"

"Symone!" Brayla yelled. "Wash your hands and come join us at the dinner table." Symone ran quickly into the dining room and took her seat. They joined hands and prayed over dinner. After dinner, they cleaned up and reconvened in the family area.

Symone pulled out a photo album and jumped in her mother's lap as they looked through the pages. Symone came across a photo of herself with a man holding her when she was a baby.

Symone asked Brayla, "Mommy, is this my daddy?"

Brayla hesitates and replies, "No, sweetie. He's just someone who was there for you when you were born."

Symone asked, "What's his name?"

The Scales of Love

"Sedric."

"Mommy, when will I get to meet my daddy?"

"God is working on that. It'll take some time, but I promise you it will happen. I love you!"

DJ picked Symone up and they headed to the park. Brayla pondered for a moment before preparing to leave for the evening.

Brayla's phone chimed as she prepared to leave. It's Bishop. She paused to read his message, "Good evening, baby. I'm sorry things have been hectic lately. Just want you to know I miss you as well. It's not just one-sided. Enjoy your evening!"

Brayla tossed her phone in her purse and headed out a little after 6:30 to meet the girls. Before she left, she moved the package from Bishop to the garage. She replayed their conversation at her office before blasting a Brian Culbertson CD and pulling off.

While cruising on I-75, her phone rings and it's Nia.

"Hey diva," Brayla said.

"Girl, I can meet ya'll, but it won't be till a little later this evening, around 8:30ish," Nia said.

"Cool," Brayla said. "See you then!"

Barakah Miller

Brayla pulled up in the parking lot and headed toward The Poetry Pit where Sasha and Amerus greeted her.

"Hey loves!" Brayla shouted.

"Girl, it's nice up in here tonight!" Amerus hollered.

"Let's sit at the bar," Sasha nudged them to come inside. "So Bray, details! It's been close to three months for you and Bishop. How is that going for the both of you?" Sasha asked as-a-matter-of-factly.

"Girl, it's great! He really has turned up his charm in wining and dining and giving a girl everything she wants, without the sex!"

"Hey," Amerus said. "That's what's up! Now how you do that?" she asked curiously.

"It's called chemistry! That, plus our history. Besides, I couldn't let him in until I felt secure enough that he was for real, for real this time. We love each other, but sometimes that's just not enough, you know?"

"I understand where you coming from. Good for you, Bray!" Sasha said, smiling.

"What about ya'll? What's going on in ya'll lives? Enough about me and Bishop."

The Scales of Love

Amerus chimed in, "Well as for me, I just closed one of the biggest deals of my career at the spa and I've been dating this guy for the last four months."

"Hey now!" Brayla shouted. "Congrats and what's his name?"

"Jason."

"You really like him, don't you? I can see it in your eyes," Brayla said.

"Yeah, I do," Amerus agreed with all smiles.

"So what's up with Sasha and Lonzo? The big entertainment guru fam," Brayla joked.

"What can I say? God is good! Lonzo's business is one of the lucrative sports and entertainment shops in its genre. He's always traveling, with me included! You know mama don't play that travel and leave wifey at home mess. Oh no, no. He knows where he goes, I go!"

The girls giggled at Sasha's fierceness.

"Hey, Nia is supposed to meet up with us around 8:30ish," Brayla informed the girls.

"That's wonderful you and Lonzo have that kind of relationship. I love your love," Amerus said.

Barakah Miller

"Awww, thanks girl. That's so sweet. I pray God's best for you and Jason," Sasha said.

"How's my God babies, Sasha?" Brayla asked.

"Grown as ever, girl you must stop by this week with the kids. Bri would love to see Symone."

"No doubt, you know that's her buddy."

"Divas!" yells Nia as she struts in, looking fabulous as ever!

"Girl, look at you," Brayla said. "You look gorgeous as always."

"Sorry for the delay, but had to take care of my boo. So what'd I miss?" Nia jumped in.

"Well..." Sasha started to bring her up-to-date on Brayla and Bishop along with Amerus's new boo.

"What..." Nia says! "Go Merus! And Bray, you working it, what can I say? Balance it! Remember, don't let his life consume your life!"

Brayla chuckled as if she was in a flashback of her conversation with Bishop and Nia earlier in the day. Brayla sighed, shaking her head saying to herself, "That must be the word of the Lord today--balancing my life and love."

10

Getting the Right Perspective

Sometimes the secret to healing is listening.

It had been three days since Bishop left. Brayla awoke to her phone chiming. She turned over and looked at the clock. It was 5:45 in the morning.

"You got to be kidding me. Who on earth is texting me at this hour! Ugh..."

She reached for her phone and it was none other than Bishop's picture flashing on her phone. "Seriously, did he forget the time zone difference?"

She opened the message, which read, "Good morning, sweetie! Sorry, if I woke you, babe! Just thinking about you. I miss you so much. Send me a sexy pic of you! Hold me over till I see you again. I love you, Bray!"

She put her phone down and turned over to get her last fifteen minutes of sleep. But her alarm went off and she immediately hit the snooze button. She closed her eyes and chanted, "My life before Bishop, always comes first!" before falling back to sleep.

The Scales of Love

Fifteen minutes go by and her alarm went off again. Brayla jumped up and said her morning prayer before heading for the shower. "What a beautiful day," Brayla said as she stretched. She looked in the mirror, said her morning confession and realized that she had not prepared to even tell Bishop about Symone. She pondered and promised herself that as soon as she got balance between her life, love and Bishop, she would bring the topic up.

"Right now, there's too much going on and I need to get to the office and make sure Symone and DJ stay in there happy place before that could ever happen anyway. No need messing up their lives," she thinks to herself.

Bray grabbed her Louis Vuitton, sunglasses and water and headed to the garage. She noticed Bishop's package sitting on the shelf.

"Hmm...I don't have time for this."

She got in her car, backed out the driveway and headed to her morning meeting. On I-75, Olivia called to remind Brayla of her lunch meeting with Tabor & Tabor.

"Oh, heck! That's Bishop's company," Brayla sighed. "I forgot about that meeting we made two months ago to go over the new development. Thanks Liv. Is the proposal complete?"

"Yes, Rico will have them waiting for you when you get there. He is the attorney assigned to work with you on this."

"Thanks, Rico is sharp. Great choice," Brayla said before disconnecting.

"Just what I need today. Okay Bray, this is not about Bishop. This is business. Besides, he's out of the country. You can rock this before he returns. It's not like he'll be at the meeting," she said to herself, entering her morning meeting.

An hour later, Brayla wrapped up her first meeting and prepared to meet with Tabor & Tabor. "Well one down, one to go," she said, walking out of her morning meeting and overjoyed of the six-figure contract she'd just nailed. "You go, Bray!" she said to herself, "What could possibly go wrong? In fact, I'm looking forward to meeting the executives at Tabor & Tabor." Brayla hopped in her car and headed to Tabor & Tabor for her meeting. As she arrived, she found Rico waiting outside to brief her before they went in.

"Hey, Ric!" Brayla said as she pulled up to valet.

"What's good, Brayla? Just wanted to brief you before we head in," Rico said. "Here is the proposal I picked up from Olivia."

The Scales of Love

"Great," Brayla said, looking over the document in the lobby. "Looks fantastic! Let's do this!"

They got on the elevator and arrived at the conference room where they were greeted by three top executives. "Hello, I'm Jalen, this is Ken and this is Michael. Glad we were able to get on your calendar, Ms. Thompson."

"Nice to meet you all," Brayla said as she introduced Rico. "This is Rico. He will be working with me on the proposal."

"Nice to meet you, Rico."

"Likewise," Rico chimed in.

"Great, please have a seat and let's get started," Jalen replied.

Brayla jumped right in and went over the proposal. Rico assisted her with answering questions and going over any legal questions. Ken and Michael were really into Brayla's presentation. Jalen got a call from his assistant letting him know that their Skype caller was on, live and ready. Jalen interrupted Brayla, "Sorry to interrupt your presentation, but one of our lead men will be joining us via Skype and he just chimed in. I apologize for the last minute notification. I hope you don't mind, but he has been working with Ken and Michael on this for quite some time."

"Sure, no problem," Brayla and Rico agreed.

"Great!" Jalen connected Bishop to the screen and confirmed, "Bishop, can you hear me?"

Brayla was in a state of shock. She almost fainted flat on her face while trying to keep her composure. She smiled and played it cool, "Shall we continue?"

"Yes," Jalen said, "please bring Bishop up to speed."

Brayla turned to the screen as Bishop lit up, trying to maintain his professionalism. "Ms. Thompson, what a joy to see you."

"Good afternoon, Mr. Moore. I was just going over the logistics of our proposal and how we can work together on the new development."

"Please proceed," Bishop replied.

Brayla got in her zone and focused in on the proposal as if she were not presenting to Bishop. Rico chimed in again to answer Bishop's legal questions and the architectural structure.

At the completion of Brayla's presentation, Ken, Michael and Jalen were thoroughly impressed with the numbers and Brayla's presentation. Ken asked Bishop, "What are your thoughts?"

"I was extremely impressed with the numbers, the architecture and the flow of logistics for this. This is my

The Scales of Love

baby. I think Ms. Thompson and Rico did a fantastic job presenting today. I say let's do it."

Brayla sighed as the team at Tabor & Tabor applauded. Rico extended his hand and shook the fellas' hands as Brayla turned around and looked at Bishop before he chimed out. He blew her a kiss and winked at her as the screen went out. Brayla, amazed at what just happened, hugged Rico as they said their goodbyes and headed for the elevator in excitement.

"Can you believe what just happened?" Rico asked Brayla in excitement. "This has got to be one of your best days. Two major deals in one day. Lady you R.O.C.K!" Rico shouted.

"Thanks Ric," Brayla said. "I'll meet you back at the office."

Brayla got in her car and headed to her office, thinking to herself, "Bishop knew all along I would be presenting on this case. He never said one word. How about that?!" She blurted out a laugh and started singing Jill Scott's Golden, "Livin my life like its golden-golden...ahh..." Brayla exhaled. "Putting it all in the right perspective."

Brayla walked into her office to a standing ovation as Rico informed the staff of the outcome of her meetings. Brayla, speechless, thanked everyone as her eyes begin to fill.

"That was so not necessary Rico, but thanks guys. You are the best staff! Without you, this wouldn't be possible. Tomorrow, lunch is on me!"

They all shouted for joy as Olivia brought Brayla a bouquet of flowers from the staff.

"Okay," Brayla said, "Friday, you're outta here at 3 p.m."

They all said in unison, "Brayla, you're the best!"

Brayla closed out her day in her office and headed home. She pulled into her garage and is once again faced with Bishop's package. She caved in and finally opened it. Within the contents of the package was a picture frame that held a picture of Bishop and Brayla with an engraved quote that read, "A couple of forevers with you are a perfect way to spend a lifetime." Brayla, astonished as her eyes filled with tears, smiled. She put the frame back in the box and entered her home.

"Mommy, mommy," Symone yelled!

"Hey babe, muah! How was your day?" Brayla asked Symone.

"It was fun. DJ's the best big bruh bruh! He took me swimming and we went to the buffet and then we went to the museum."

The Scales of Love

"Boy, you guys had a blast today. Thanks big man," Brayla said to DJ.

"Mom, you don't have to thank me. She's my sister. I'd do anything for that little girl."

"I know," Brayla said. "But I know you're trying to get ready for college as well."

"Mom, it's no big deal," DJ insisted.

As Brayla took a seat in the living room, the doorbell rang. DJ got it.

"Hey mom, it's for you," DJ yelled.

Brayla wondered who it could be as she staggered into the foyer. She looked up to see Sedric.

"OMG!"

"Hello, Brayla," Sedric said. "Long time no see!"

"When did you get back?" Brayla asked in disbelief, standing in front of Sedric's 6'2" muscular frame all decked out in Army attire.

"I just flew in today on two weeks leave."

"That's great. I'm sorry Sedric, you got me at a bad time," Brayla gestured.

Sedric said, "No, forgive me for dropping in unannounced."

"Yeah, something with the exes. They just have a way of poppin' up…" Brayla said under her voice.

Time Out for Love

If you're not taking care of you, who will?

It's Friday and DJ and Symone are off to a weekend with Sasha and her family. While Brayla prepared for a long relaxing weekend of R & R, her cell phone rang. She continued to prepare for her spa appointment while looking at the phone. It was Sedric.

"Hello, Bray. How's your morning?"

"Fabulous!" she responded. "I'm on my way out for an appointment – what's up?"

"I was hoping you would join me for a late lunch."

Brayla shook her head, thinking to herself, "I knew this was coming. Sedric, thanks for the invitation, but I have a full weekend already planned."

"Well, would you please reconsider? If not this weekend, at least before I head back?"

"I'm sure I can do that, Sedric. I'll let you know when I'm available."

The Scales of Love

"Why is this happening to me? What is up with the exes? I'm just going to enjoy my day with no thoughts or communication with any exes. This is my day," Brayla said as she entered the spa.

Amerus walked up to Brayla as she entered the spa.

"Girl, I didn't know you were coming today! You should have called me last night and I would have reserved the VIP room for you."

"No big deal," Brayla replied. "Girl, I need a massage – badly!"

"I'm at your service. Are you getting your usual as well?" Amerus asked Brayla.

"Yes," Brayla responded as Amerus motioned one of her staff to assist Brayla.

"No worries, girl. This one's on the house."

"Thanks Merus," Brayla said as she proceeded to her massage.

"Oh yes, this is just what I needed!" exclaimed Brayla! Brayla fell into a temporarily deep sleep as her body relaxed to the flow of her massage. "Whoa! I must have been super tight," Brayla said as she is awakened.

The masseuse says, "Yes you were."

"Thanks, awesome job!"

Brayla got dressed and headed for a facial prior to getting her mani and pedi done. As she relaxed in the massage chair, she saw Nyla walk in with her daughters. Brayla and Nyla made eye contact briefly. Brayla put her head back on her chair and closed her eyes. She sighed, "Wow!"

Amerus walked over and asked Brayla if everything was to her liking and if she could get her anything. Brayla smiled and said, "You know your staff is the bomb.com! Thanks, but I'm just about finished here."

"Are you sure? It's not a problem. You know I love catering to my customers!"

"And that you do a fabulous job at," Brayla agreed. "Stop by after work."

"Will do!"

Brayla tipped the staff and left. While she proceeded to her car, Sedric called again. She sent him to voicemail and drove off. She stopped at The Detroit Seafood Market and ran into Rico at the bar.

"Hey beautiful," Rico said as he greeted Brayla.

"Hey Ric! What are you doing here...solo at that?" Brayla asked, smiling.

The Scales of Love

"Just hanging out for a moment. What about you?"

"Just finished a little R & R and I stopped by for a quick bite to take home."

"Well, may I join you instead of your take-out?" he offered.

"Yes, I like that."

They got a table and placed their orders.

"We haven't had this in a very long time," Brayla said.

"That's because you always play me short."

Brayla laughed, "What are you talking about dude?"

"You know exactly what I'm talking about," he said. "You and all your rules. 'No intimate relationships with your employees or colleagues,'" he mimicked Brayla.

"Works for me. That's really doing too dang much. Never mix business with pleasure - throws you off."

"I must disagree," Rico said.

"I'm sure you would," Brayla chuckled. "Oh and for the record, this is not a date!"

"Whoever said it was!"

"You're so darn charming – it's ridiculous! Where's your other half?"

"I'll be meeting her this evening. She's great."

Their food arrived and they toasted and enjoyed conversation for a few hours before departing ways.

Brayla arrived home as Amerus called and said she'd be stopping by close to 9 p.m. Brayla went upstairs to refresh and relax in her chaise when she noticed messages on her voicemail. She was hesitant to check them, afraid they were from Bishop or Sedric. Against her better judgment, she checked them anyway. The first message was from Symone, followed by messages from Bishop and Sedric.

Brayla smiled as she heard Symone's message. "Hi Mommy, just calling to say I love you!"

Bishop's messages weren't far behind. "Hey baby, it's your baby Bishop! I was thinking about you and I'll be back early. I was hoping to see you once I got in. Give me a call or text later and let me know. I miss you. Bye baby!"

There was another message. "Hello Bray, I called you the other day. I haven't heard from you. I'm leaving you a message so you know that I called. Give me a call when you can. Okay, bye baby."

Then, came Sedric's message. "Hi Bray! I don't mean to bother you, but I only have a short amount of time before I head back on duty. I would really like to spend some time with you prior to me leaving. Give me a call. I'm staying at my cousin's. I'll await your response."

Brayla picked up her remote and pressed PLAY as the soft, sensual sounds of Will Downing and Gerald Albright played in the background. She relaxed in her chaise, closed her eyes and exhaled before saying, "For the love of Brayla."

12

Taking Control

The tasks ahead of you are never greater than the strength within you.

It's 8:45 in the evening and Brayla's in the kitchen making virgin daiquiris for her and Amerus with light appetizers. The doorbell rang. Brayla walked toward the foyer, assuming it was Amerus. She opens the door.

"Hey lady!" Amerus said, smiling.

"Come on in girl. I made daiquiris, would you like one?"

"Fo sho. After my day, I'm exhausted."

"Yeah, you were busy today shortie, especially for a Friday," Brayla hollered from the kitchen. "So, no evening plans with Jason?"

"No, not tonight. I don't think I would be up for it anyway as tired as I am," Amerus sighed.

"Girl, that's one thing you got to learn. No matter how tired we get, we always got to find time for love. Remember our conversation? We may not be up for it, but if he wants to go out and hang or have dinner or even make love, we as women have to inconvenience ourselves to accommodate them. It's called compromise."

"Well, I guess I'm just not ready for all that loveish. Shoot, I'm tired. I'm tired! Period! He just gone have to man up, put on his big man briefs and suck it up!" They both laughed.

Brayla said, "Girl, you are too much. Young, gorgeous and so much to learn!"

"That's alright – that's what I have my divas for." Amerus took a sip of her drink and reached for an appetizer. "Mmm...girl these appetizers are the bomb!"

"Thanks boo."

"So I saw that eye contact thing you and Mrs. Nyla had going on at the shop. What was that about?"

"Just a little informal greeting, that's all," Brayla said with an awkward smile.

"Yeah, whatever B," Amerus said. "It was brief, but I sensed it was more to it than you're telling."

"Nope not at all," Brayla changed the subject. "So guess who popped up the other day at my front door?"

"Who?" Amerus asked in a curious tone.

"Sedric!"

"Girl, no! When did he get back?"

"I guess that day. He's on leave for two weeks and he wants us to spend some quality time together before he goes back."

"Girl, Bishop ain't gone go for that. You already know. By the way, is he back?"

"Not yet. He left a message stating he'll be back early so I'm assuming one day this week."

"You didn't call him back?"

"Nope!"

"Huh? Okay girl, what's really going on with you and your love life?" Amerus inquired.

"I'm just putting things in perspective and taking care of Brayla for once. You know aligning my wants and my worth...my life comes first before any man. Especially since I don't have a ring – they all can take a back seat."

"So when did all this come about?"

"Girl, life in general. I just have to find a balance within my life, love and Bishop, if he's going to be the man to occupy my time."

The Scales of Love

"Alrighty then!" Amerus shouted as she held up her glass to toast with Brayla. "Here's to Bray!"

"I like that!" Brayla said.

"Well girl, I must be movin' my tired, sexy behind home. We'll chat soon."

"Thanks for stopping by hon'. Call or text me so I know you made it home safely," Brayla said.

"I will."

The next morning, Brayla decided to return Sedric's call and let him know that she could meet him Tuesday for an early brunch before heading to her office. She also instructed Sedric not to make any more unannounced visits without calling first.

He agreed and apologized immediately with a simplistic, "I understand."

Brayla headed to her patio to take up some sun and relax by the pool. As she's was reading, her phone chimed. It was Bishop.

She answered, "Hello love."

"Hey baby, it's good to hear your voice. How have you been? Miss me yet?"

"Naw, not yet. Just kidding, I'm well babe. What about you? How's business?"

"I'm better now that I hear my angel's voice," Bishop said. "Man, I can't wait to see you! I'll be in early this week."

"That's great B! So guess who I ran into this weekend?"

"Who?" Bishop asked.

"Your wife and she had the girls with her."

"Really," Bishop said, a little timid.

"Bishop, you sound surprised. In case you're wondering, and I know you are, we didn't speak, just a little eye contact that's all. You never cease to amaze me."

"What's that supposed to mean? Cause I didn't give you the reaction you wanted?"

"Bishop, please. Don't give yourself more credit than you deserve."

"What the heck is that supposed to mean Bray?"

"Nothin'. I'm glad you called baby. We'll talk soon."

"Bray, I know you're not rushing me off the phone!"

"Enjoy your flight love. Bye, Bishop," Brayla said as she hung up the phone.

The Scales of Love

Brayla continued her reading and came across a quote from Viktor Frankl which read, "When we can no longer change a situation, we are challenged to change ourselves." Brayla pondered on that for a moment and realized that she needed major changes in her life and she had to do it on purpose.

"Wow! For six years, I have allowed this man to control this entire relationship. When we see each other, how often we're together, and where we see each other, if at all. No one should have that kind of power or control over any relationship. This is supposed to be a mutual relationship based on friendship. The majority say has been in his favor and not mine. Seriously, Brayla?! As much as I want to believe Bishop and how he feels about me, his actions have spoken for him. God is supposed to be the head of all my relationships. I see He has hidden His face from me on this one. Well Father, the message has been delivered."

Brayla closed her book and headed into her bedroom where she picked up the frame Bishop sent before he left. She re-read the engraved quote: "A couple of forevers with you are a perfect way to spend a lifetime." Brayla paused and thought out loud, "How can someone so kind, gentle and sincere be such an ass at the same time?" She threw the frame on her bed and headed for the shower.

As Brayla stood in front of her mirror putting her hair up, she said to herself, "Girl, you have got to get it together.

Barakah Miller

Don't allow your heart, emotions, or love to keep you in hell. He's never going to change. He's never going to leave her. He may very well love you and all that other stuff. At the end of the day, he's there with her and their babies, sharing their house, blitzen in their love, in their bed. Bray, you'll never get a man to commit to you under those circumstances! And that's my reality." She got into the shower.

13

Embracing Brayla

Giving up on something good for something better!

On Sunday evening, Brayla picked up her kids from Lonzo's and Sasha's house. Symone saw Brayla pulling up and ran outside to greet her.

"Mommy, mommy!" Symone screamed, excited to see her.

Brayla grabbed her purse and locked her car. She greeted Symone with hugs and kisses.

"Oh, how I missed you Monie!" Brayla exclaimed.

"I missed you too, mommy!"

"Did you enjoy your God-family?"

"Yes, we had so much fun," Symone said, eager to tell Brayla of her extensive weekend.

"Where's Godma Sasha at?"

"On the patio in the back."

The Scales of Love

"Cool, walk mommy to the back."

"Hello, hello peeps!" Brayla shouted.

"What's up sista girl," Lonzo said in excitement, hugging Brayla. "I haven't seen you in a minute."

"I know, it's been awhile world traveler. How many miles on your pass?" Brayla said jokingly. Everyone laughed.

"Hey Bray," Sasha said.

"My sista, how are you? Girl, I know you gots to be tired, keeping up with all these babies this weekend," Brayla said.

"Bray, you know they keep me fine and on my toes. I can roll wit'em. What about you? No kids this weekend. What you get into?

"Not a dang thang girl. Just some R & R and quality time with me."

"I heard that," Lonzo said, joining in on their conversation. "You got us next weekend right?" Lonzo joked.

"I got you boo, but not next weekend," Brayla smiled. Lonzo embraced Sasha then headed into the house.

"So Amerus tells me Sedric's back," Sasha chimed in.

"That would be correct – temporarily."

"So are you going to meet up with him?"

"Yeah, I told him I'd meet him one day this week before my appointments."

"And what do you think Bishop will say?"

"What can he say," Brayla bellowed. "I'm not worried about Bishop. I have my life and he has his."

"Mmmm...where's that coming from?" Sasha asked, sounding a little confused. "Amerus said you were on an 'all about Brayla' party train."

"Yes, I am and if you don't like it, move out the way," Brayla said as-a-matter- of-factly. "Seriously," Brayla said, "I just got to get back to me. I need to focus on me, my kids, my businesses, my relationship with God, my life altogether. All that extra stuff is last on the list."

"Bray, I'm a little confused. Don't get me wrong, that's great, but I thought what you said you wanted was to get back with Bishop? The love I witnessed between y'all is deep. What happened to that? You don't just give up on love like that, as hard as it is to find real authentic genuine love. Bray, what are you really holding back on – for real?"

"Sasha, I can't deny that what I feel for Bishop is as real as a hurricane. But lately, I've had to put all that into perspective."

The Scales of Love

"Meaning what? Are you considering leaving him for good?"

"I don't know. Maybe," Brayla said in a soft, low tone.

"Girl, is it that bad? You just said the other night things are going well and Bishop is doing all the right things."

"Girl, there's so much more to our relationship than us being in love," Brayla said, walking over to the cooler for a drink.

"Ok," Sasha said, "let's just stop right there. That one's on a need-to-know basis and I don't need to know, nor do I want to."

"Thanks for respecting the privacy."

"You ain't got to thank me. I know how relationships can go and sometimes love, no matter how much you love a person, is not always enough to keep any flame burning."

"Ain't that the truth? It's getting late. Let me round up my babies."

Brayla called for her kids and they all said their goodbyes. Symone told Brayla all about her weekend on the ride home. Brayla pulled up in their driveway twenty minutes later. The children jumped out and headed toward the house.

Barakah Miller

Brayla told DJ to run Symone's bath and told him to get ready for bed as well as she headed to her bedroom. The first thing she saw was the picture frame she left on her bed as she walked toward her bed to lie down. Brayla picked up the frame and embraced it as she thought of all the love in her heart for Bishop. Tears rolled down her face as images of Bishop resurfaced. She could hear the sound of his voice in the back of her head.

She cried into the midnight hour, embracing the frame and looking intently at the photo within the frame. She read the quote one last time before closing her eyes and said, "You are my one true love, my heart, my joy, my sunshine. But no matter how much we may love each other, we cannot be together. I love me more!"

14

Accepting Accountability

When we realize life is not about us, that's when our responsibility kicks in!

On Monday morning, Brayla woke up at the top of her game as she headed out to meet Nia for breakfast. She arrived at IHOP and met Nia inside.

"Good morning, sister," Nia said as she greeted Brayla.

"Hey sis, glad we could meet this morning."

"Me too."

The hostess seated them and Nia said, "Okay Bray, what's going on?"

"I love you girl," Brayla said, smiling. "You know Nia, I always thought Bishop and I had something special. I know we've had several break-ups on and off over the course of six years, but I never took the opportunity to really reflect on our entire relationship. I mean, had I not been so insanely emotional and really listened to what he was saying outside of what I just wanted to hear, see, and feel, maybe things would be different now. He said some things that really made sense and I, being on the other side of the fence, would always take them the wrong way, as if he was tryna play me or hurt me. Honestly, I always thought somewhere in our relationship, he was always trying to get over."

Brayla paused to regain her composure.

"I know within my heart that was never his intention. But I always had my guard up – always! I was so afraid he was going to hurt me and considering our relationship as it is, that had a lot to do with it. I never realized how much of the old I was still holding onto until I was faced with a challenge within our relationship. When those old, too-familiar emotions rose up, I automatically put him in the same category and my defense instantly kicked in. I never gave him a fair chance because I was always afraid of being the one to get hurt or ending up without him, or ending up with nothing after investing so much into us. Kinda felt as if I was battling demons in regards to my father abandoning me; so here I am once again sabotaging my relationship and making unhealthy choices. Him being married never made it any easier, either. You know the day you dread to hear, "Things are getting better over the course of the years I just couldn't tell you because my love for you, still so very much remains." Those words hurt so much to hear."

Brayla used a napkin from the table to wipe her tears.

Barakah Miller

"Girl, yes. He went there. Yet, he still turned around and came back. And me being a fool for love--I let him. I hate when he texts me and expects me to read between the lines and assume I get it. Ain't nobody got time for all that! Just say it! Heck, I may miss something. Just tell me what's between the lines so I can understand where you're coming from. Don't assume anything because when you do, you allow miscommunication to set in. Oh, and don't think I'm about to hold a full conversation with you via text. I'm sorry. I'm old school. If you have that much to say, you better hit me up on the phone...period! Respect me enough to verbally communicate with me. I want to hear how you feel, not read it. However, for the most part, he has always been upfront. But then he started holding things back. So I would ponder what I was doing and most of the time, it wasn't even me. Girl, I'm sorry! I'm over here just venting!"

Nia said, "Go right ahead. I'm only hear to listen, remember?"

Brayla smiled and exhaled, "Thanks Nia!"

The server came and they placed their order. Brayla took a sip of her water before proceeding, "I must admit, this past weekend I have been reflecting and I had to come to the realization that I have to accept my part in all this. It's not just on him. Heck, it's not even about him. I accept my part and I take full ownership of my emotions and the part I have played in our relationship. You know, sometimes I look at him and all I see is a married man. Knowing things are not going to get any better or change, no matter what he says. But now, I can't get past the fact that he's married and that blocks everything. I can't see any clearer than that!"

Nia reached for Brayla's hand and said, "Good for you! I'm so proud of you girl. That's a big step. You know I'm here for you and I would never judge you, nor have I ever. Trust me, it's going to get better. I know it's still going to take a little more time to tell Bishop how you feel, but it won't be as hard as you are imaging it will be. I promise you that."

"Girl, that's not the part I'm concerned about," Brayla said in a low-spirited tone.

Nia said, "Bray, what are you referring to?"

Brayla chimed in and said, "You remember Sedric?"

Nia replied, "Yes, I heard he's here for a visit. What does he have to do with all this?"

"Well, I met him when I was three months pregnant. I never said anything because everybody assumed Symone was his and I never imaged me and Bishop getting back together, so I never said anything. I know that was misleading, but Sedric didn't mind so…"

"Brayla!" Nia shouted. "Are you telling me Symone is Bishop's daughter?"

"Yes."

"OMG!" Nia cried out loud.

"No one else knows but DJ, and of course Sedric," Brayla continued. "Sedric and I never talked about Bishop. He never asked any questions, so I never volunteered any answers. That was a part of my life I didn't want to revisit and he respected that."

"So what now?" Nia asked persistently. "You are going to tell him, right? I can't believe Bishop hasn't put two and two together. I mean, y'all got right back together a few months after Sedric left and he's not once said anything?"

"I know, right? I don't really have much of a choice. Symone has been asking about her father and if it was up to me, I would leave things the way they are. But I can't do that to my baby. She, as well as Bishop, both have a right to know regardless of how I may feel."

"Well, I must say I'm glad you got your head on straight in regards to telling him the truth about Symone. Girl," Nia said, shaking her head, "God will be with you, but you got some housekeeping to do."

"No need to remind me," Brayla contended. "Holding myself accountable is great. It's just when the situation is cloudy, that's when I come to realize how much resilience I have. I also come to know that sometimes the secret to healing is listening. Bishop has always been very adamant about certain things. He always repeated them in some form. I would have been in a much better place than where I am now. I'm not blaming myself for anything, just the one life lesson I have learned. When a man shows you who he is, believe him."

"Girl, I know you're afraid to tell him, considering his past comments. But that's just one situation his black behind just gone have to deal with. Period! It's not like you slipped and fell on his dick! You both are two mature individuals, fully aware of your actions. Now, it's time for him to man up and accept his part as well, regardless how dang stressful it may be!" Nia said furiously.

"What was your breaking point when you realized you were over your ex?"

"The breaking point for me was when nothing was working for me. I had tried everything and nothing worked. But when I was really at peace, then I knew because nothing he did or said fazed me anymore. You know what God has in store for you, only the best! Somebody totally for you and totally yours."

"Tell that to my heart! I know. I'm focused on keeping it positive. Just don't want it lingering in my mind or heart."

"I know the heart is what gets us in the most trouble. But that is when only God can help. And I promise He knows where you are."

"Thanks girl for everything. I got to get to work. We'll meet up soon," Brayla said.

"You enjoy the rest of your day and don't let this alter your mood. You're way to gorgeous to be walking around with a frown on your face," Nia reassured her.

Brayla arrived back at the office. Upon entering her office, she noticed six vases full of purple roses. She instantly knew they were from Bishop. She walked in her office and closed the door. She put her things on the couch and grabbed one of the cards from the roses, reading it aloud, "You are the epitome of beauty! Your love for me has made me a better man. You forever have my heart! –Bishop" She walked over and read another card, "I could never express my love for you in words. You are the true embodiment of love." Brayla reached for the third card, which said, "You are the light to my soul, the one whom I love to love to love!"

Brayla stopped and paused before saying, "He is not going to make this any easier." She tossed the cards on her desk and started her workday.

15

A Heavy Heart

When the issues of life begin to take a toll, seek God!

Later that evening, Brayla arrived home, kicked off her stilettos and crashed on the couch. "What a day," she muttered. She picked up her mail and shuffled through it. The phone rang and, of course, it was Bishop.

"Hello."

"Hey love," Bishop replied back.

"Hey handsome! I got a beautiful display of purple roses today. Thank you babe. I can't express to you what that meant to me. Not just the display. I'm referring to all six of your messages!"

"The last six years with you have been a little rocky, but you consistently stayed by my side regardless of what I was going through or what we experienced. You have been there for me in my darkest moments. I could never repay you for your generosity and the love you have always given and shown toward me. You love me for me...unconditionally. You are truly my love!"

Brayla paused, creating an extended moment of silence.

Bishop said, "Hello Bray?"

"Yes, I'm still here. Bishop, listen. I know you love me and as we both said in the past, we don't know what the future holds. I need you to be aware that I too have a heart and what I've always felt for you came straight from my heart. I know my worth and the value within my heart and if there is any inkling of a thought that you know we're not going to seriously work on us – don't continue to romance me."

"Bray, where is this coming from? I have no intentions on going anywhere. I plan on us getting back close. You got me!"

"Okay," Brayla said in a firm voice. "Babe, I just got in not too long ago and I just need to be by myself for a little bit before the kids come in."

"What's going on with you Bray? You've been sounding a little distanced lately. Tell me baby, what's on your mind?"

"I've just been doing some self-reevaluation, that's all B," Brayla reassured him.

"I hope you know you can talk to me about anything baby."

"I know boo, I know. But, I gotta go. We'll talk or see each other later this week when you get back. Love you."

"I love you, too. We'll talk soon baby."

Shortly after, the kids came in. "Hi mom," Symone and DJ said in unison.

"Hey babies! How was camp, Symone?"

"I had a blast! We went swimming at the water park and had a picnic," Symone said, joyfully explaining her day. "We did face painting too mommy!"

"I see you have your face all dolled up. And what about you, DJ? How was your day?"

"Relaxing! I had fun chaperoning Symone at the water park and then I went and played hoops. How was work?"

"Busy! I'm so tired today. I guess take out or pizza is on the table for dinner. You guys pick which one you want and let me know and I got you. I'm way too tired to cook tonight," Brayla said, yawning. "I think I'ma head to bed early."

"Dang mom," DJ said. "You must be super whipped. It's only 6:30 p.m."

"Baby yes. Plus I've got a lot on my mind. I'll leave the money on the table for your dinner. Smooches! See you loves in the morning," Brayla said as she headed to her bedroom.

"Good night, mommy," Symone said.

Brayla said a prayer then climbed into her bed, falling into a deep sleep. Throughout the night, images of her relationship with Bishop entered her mind as she slept. She tossed and turned throughout the night until finally, she awakened. She jumped up out of her sleep with a look of distress, turned to look at the clock and noticed it was 3 in the morning.

She fell back down on her pillows, looking up. She turned over and opened her night stand, pulling out the frame from Bishop. She dazed at the photo and began to cry as she softly started a conversation with God.

"Father, take the pain away. I love him so much. Love is not supposed to hurt or be like this. I know this is not right and I'm sorry! Please forgive me and give me the strength to walk away. I don't think I'm strong enough to do this on my own. Daddy God, I need you! Lord, help Bishop become a better man. Search his heart and his mind. Strengthen him to be a better husband and father. Equip him to lead his family. I pray 3 John 1-2 over him. Show me how to communicate with him the truth about Symone. I'm afraid! I've always been afraid of that moment and losing him – completely out my life. I'm afraid of being abandoned by the man I love, just as my father abandoned me. Why must

Barakah Miller

I always sabotage my relationships, especially when it comes to love? What's wrong with me? Lord, show me how you see me, how you value me, and how you love me. Show me how to align my worth and my wants. I don't know why or what is happening to me, but I don't want to be afraid anymore. I want to trust you. God, do for me what I can't do for myself. God I need you."

She sobbed louder, "God I need you!"

16

Taking Care of Business

When juggling life, love and business, you must put your priorities in order.

On Tuesday morning, Brayla rolled out of bed to prepare for work. She pulled out her tablet and checked her calendar for the day. She noticed that she has an early brunch appointment with Sedric. She looked at the clock and realized that she should have been on her way to meet him. She grabbed her phone and called Sedric.

"Hey Sedric. It's Brayla. Just want you to know I'm on my way. I should be there in about 10 minutes."

"I look forward to seeing you."

Brayla gathered her things and walked out the door. She arrived at the restaurant and had valet park her car as she headed in to meet Sedric. Sedric saw Brayla walking in and stood up to greet her.

"Good morning," Sedric said with a smile.

"How are you, Sedric?"

"I'm glad you agreed to meet me. So I'm not going to waste your time. I know you have a lot going on this morning, so I'm just going to dive right in."

"Please, go right ahead," Brayla urged.

"Brayla, we were together for a year prior to me being deported. I was there at the birth of Symone and I just feel the connection we have is still there. What I'm saying is I want us to try again. I feel like a part of that little girl is me, and I want you to consider dating me for marriage."

Brayla choked on her water, "Excuse me," she struggled to say. "Did you say marriage?! Sedric, that's a lot to ask a girl this early in the morning. Honestly, Sedric I can't and I won't consider. I have way too much going on in my life right now to even entertain that."

Sedric persisted, "Would you please at least just think about it?"

"Sedric, I can't think about it and give you an answer before you leave. I have other things on my mind at the moment that outweigh your proposal. It wouldn't be fair to you. Sedric, I'm trying to be upfront with you and not mislead you to think otherwise. I can't consider," Brayla asserted.

Barakah Miller

Brayla grabbed her bag and told Sedric it was nice seeing him as she proceeded to leave. Valet pulled up with her car as her phone chimed. It was a text from Bishop. "Where's my baby at?"

Brayla tossed her phone in the seat and drove off. She arrived at the garage, pulled into her parking space and pulled out her tablet to check the numbers on her boutique before heading up to the office to meet up with Rico.

She saw Olivia pulling up, so she closed out her tablet and greeted Olivia in the parking lot. They rode the elevator together.

"Morning, Ms. Thompson," Olivia said.

"Morning to you as well, Liv. How was your training?"

"It was good. Thanks so much for putting me down to go. I really learned a lot."

"Great, I'm glad you went. Enjoy the rest of your day," Brayla said as she passed Olivia's desk and walked into her office.

Brayla put her things on the couch and grabbed her notebook as Rico walked in for their meeting.

"Ms. Thompson, are you ready to meet?"

"Sure, have a seat Rico."

The Scales of Love

Rico came in and closed the door behind him. Brayla informed Rico that she was giving him the lead on the new development project and that he would be reporting back to her. She told him that she was also assigning Dennis from engineering to assist him. She reiterated that with his legal and business background, the duo should work great as a team.

Rico assured Ms. Thompson that she could trust him with this and that he was looking forward to meeting his new partner. They adjourn and Brayla proceeded to make some calls. While Brayla was on the phone, she heard her cell phone chiming again. She ignored it, but it chimed yet again... and again. Irritated, Brayla put her call on speaker, walked over to the couch and picked up her phone.

Two messages from Bishop flashed across her screen. She laid her phone on her desk and continued her business call. Olivia buzzed her to remind her of her conference call with Tabor & Tabor. Brayla ended her current call and buzzed Rico and Dennis to her office to sit in on the call.

Olivia buzzed Brayla again to inform her that Tabor & Tabor were on the line and ready. Brayla connected them and said, "Good morning Ken, Jalen and Michael."

"Good morning Brayla," they all replied.

Brayla informed them that Rico was taking the lead on the development and that Dennis, their lead engineer and architect, would be assisting him.

Michael chimed in, "Brayla, we were hoping to work directly with you. Considering your record, we selected you assuming you would be leading on this."

Brayla assured the Tabor & Tabor team that they were in great hands and that Rico would be reporting directly back to her. Furthermore, if they had any further concerns, she had an open-door policy.

Ken replied, "Okay, Ms. Thompson. We will trust you on this one. Rico and Dennis, we'll see you bright and early Thursday morning."

Rico and Dennis replied, "We are looking forward to working with you all."

They ended the call, and Rico and Dennis exited Brayla's office.

Brayla picked up her cell phone and read Bishop's messages. "I'm back home boo! I wanna see you baby." She read his second message. "I am truly missing you!" She sat her cell phone to the side as she pondered whether or not to respond to his messages. Her thoughts were interrupted with a visit from Nia.

The Scales of Love

"Hey girl," Nia said. "I thought I'd pop in and check on you and bring you your fav chai latte."

"Ooo baby girl, just what I needed. Thanks!"

"So what's up with you? How are you doing, Bray?"

"I'm holding on. Sometimes, I don't know if I'm coming or going. So overwhelmed with all this emotional drama. I'll be happy when this is all over and I can get back to me!"

"Girl, I told you there was a price that came with your decision. Now you're just going to have to let it all play out," Nia reminded her.

"I know, Nia. I'm just a little afraid of the outcome, that's all. Just the thought of telling him fills me up with tears."

"Bray, it's going to be okay. From here on out, you got to just trust God baby."

"You're right, I just keep thinking of those words Bishop said last time we faced this situation, 'We both know that's not what we want (a baby)...I don't need that kind of stress in my life...ever!' You know Nia, men are a trip. When they slip up and get caught up in the moment, it's okay. But when we do it, it's a double standard! Men are so full of themselves. Girl I've got to get back to work. Thanks for the tea and the talk. I appreciate you more than you know girl." Brayla smiled and hugged Nia.

"You know I'm here for you," Nia said. "Anytime, any hour!"

"Thanks Nia!"

Nia walked out of Brayla's office and headed toward the elevator. Brayla picked up her phone and texted Bishop back, "I just got all three of your messages. I'm in the office. Let's meet up later."

Later that evening, Brayla realized that Bishop never responded back to her message, so she texted him again. "Hey babe, did you get my message earlier?"

A few minutes later, Bishop responded, "Yep! I've been workin' like a slave since I got back to the office. Call you soon."

Brayla sighed, "Here we go!"

17

Family First

Setting your priorities concerning love requires you to put your family first.

DJ was in the living room waiting on his mother to come downstairs for their routine family meeting. Symone walked in and sat down on the couch next to DJ. Brayla arrived shortly after.

"Hey babies. Let's pray before we start." Brayla instructed DJ to lead them into prayer. They all stood up and held hands as DJ started.

"Heavenly Father, we come to you with humble hearts and thanksgiving. We ask that you will embrace our mother with the wisdom to continue leading us. Bless her hands and all of her businesses. Dear Lord, protect her and shield her so that no hurt, harm nor danger comes near her. Strengthen our bond as a family and lead us continually on the path of righteousness. Lord, we love you and our hearts seek your ways daily. Lord, lead my steps toward your will. Holy Spirit, rise up and help me to make the right decision for my future. And lastly, Father, give my little sister Symone the comfort, joy, peace and reassurance that the only daddy she needs is in you. In Jesus' name, amen!"

"Wow DJ," Symone said. "That was an awesome prayer!"

Brayla, taken back by the words her son just prayed, was speechless as a tear drop fell from her cheek. "DJ, God is definitely using you baby," Brayla said, smiling at DJ. DJ smiled and nodded as Brayla began speaking to them about the coming year.

"Well, we all know and are very much excited that DJ will soon be on his way to college. DJ, have you made your final appointments to view U of M and Iowa?"

"Yes, we are all set to go in the morning to Michigan to talk with the coach one last time and then I'm off with Uncle Lonzo to Iowa to revisit."

"Man, I am so very proud of you," Brayla continued. "You are handling your business and seeking God to assist you in the process. Remember to always keep Him in the mix and seek His guidance, baby."

"I will ma'am," DJ assured her.

"So how long will you have to make your decision when you come back?"

"Well with Unc by my side, I was hoping he would pray with me one last time before I make that final decision. I would like to have my decision by the end or beginning of next week, if not sooner. I am running out of time," DJ sighed.

"Well, we all are here for you and whatever you decide, we got your back," Brayla comforted him with a smile and moved on to Symone. "Well, I guess that leaves little Ms. Symone next on the agenda."

Symone, extremely excited, said, "I'm listening mommy!"

"As for you young lady, you will be starting your new school this year as well as dance, swimming and gymnastics."

Symone yelled, "Yes!"

"Ms. Olivia from my office will be assisting me in transporting you to your after-school activities. In the fall, you will begin dance and after Christmas, you'll start gymnastics and lastly, swimming. Tomorrow you'll go with me to visit your new school."

"Oh boy, I can't wait!" Symone shouted.

"Now, here's an update on mommy." She proceeded to tell them about the six-figure contract she got for her boutique and the new development with Tabor & Tabor. She informed them that her work schedule was more than likely going to pick up, but reassured them that family time would not be adjusted.

DJ chimed in, "Mama Dukes, I'm so proud of you. You doin' the dang thang little Ms. Business Woman of the Year!" They chuckle and fall into a group hug. "Wow, I can't believe you got that deal with Bishop's company. How you pull that off? They're one of the prominent companies in the country!" DJ said.

"God," she immediately replied. "Plus, that proposal. I worked my butt off putting it together with Rico. Let's celebrate! Who's all in?" Brayla asked.

DJ and Symone both yelled, "I'll beat you to the car!"

Symone yelled, "Shotgun!"

They arrived at the Capitol Grille and were seated by the hostess. They placed their order for their drinks and Brayla looked up just in time to see Bishop entering with his wife.

"Just what my eyes needed to see," Brayla said to herself. Bishop and Nyla were seated on the other side of the restaurant in Brayla's view. Brayla murmured, "Just what I needed to ruin my night. It's all good." She changed her composure, smiled at her kids and paid extra attention as the server approached her table for their order. They ordered and Symone said she had to use the restroom.

Brayla said, "God, this is not the time for your sense of humor."

Brayla grabbed Symone's hand as they proceeded to the restroom, which was kiddy corner from Bishop's table.

Bishop got a quick view of a woman whom he thought looked a lot like Brayla. He said to himself, "Dang, not tonight," under his breath.

Nyla said, "What did you say?"

"Nothing."

Brayla and Symone exited the restroom with their backs turned toward Bishop, so he still was not able to confirm if the woman was Brayla or not. Bishop, now on edge, excused himself to the restroom. He pulled out his phone and texted Brayla, hoping she would respond back. "Hey babe, where you at?"

Brayla's sees her phone buzz with the incoming message from Bishop. She ignored it. He texted her again anxiously, knowing he had to get back to his wife.

"Come on Bray, answer me...dang! Bray, why aren't you responding to me?!"

Brayla got his message the second time and fell out laughing. She said to herself, "Are you busting a sweat? That's what yo behind gets." She ignored the texts again as she focused on her family and not the love triangle Bishop insisted on creating.

Bishop walked out of the restroom and looked across the restaurant, hoping to confirm that the woman he briefly saw was in fact Brayla. He returned to his seat a little confused. Nyla asked him what took him so long.

He replied, "I was waiting on a wine list."

Nyla looked at him in disbelief and said, "Are you okay? You look a little disoriented. What's wrong?"

"Nothing babe, I'm cool," Bishop reassured her.

Upon Brayla's departure from the restaurant, she texted Bishop back, "Yes, I see you." She walked out the door with her children.

18

Morning Shuffle

Putting your priorities in order requires a commitment to yourself!

The next morning, Brayla got up to see DJ off with Lonzo while she got Symone ready for her school visit. Symone came downstairs, hugged DJ and jumped into Lonzo's arms and gave him a giant hug. Symone told her Godfather to take care of her 'bruh bruh' and to be careful. Lonzo assured Symone that he'd bring DJ back just the way he left. He kissed her on the forehead as DJ and he walked out the door.

Symone headed to the kitchen for breakfast as Brayla finished a call from the office. Brayla asked Symone if she was almost ready.

Symone replied, "Soon as I'm done with breakfast."

"Great," Brayla responded as she loaded the car.

Brayla looked over her shoulder and noticed Sedric sitting outside her house in his car. She closed her car door and walked out to his car. She tapped on his window. He rolled it down and Brayla said, "I thought I told you no more pop up visits?!"

Sedric responds, "I apologize. I got called back sooner than expected and I leave tonight. I just wanted to see you and Symone before I leave if that's okay with you Bray?"

Brayla adjusted her demeanor in the calmest way and said, "You could have called and asked me that, Sedric. I have an appointment I'm getting ready for and I do not appreciate you dropping by unannounced! I'll have to think about that but right now, I have to get Symone so we're not late."

Sedric yelled, "Brayla wait!"

Brayla paused as Sedric proceeded, "I know you have a lot on your plate and I don't mean to add any more stress to that. Is what I'm really asking that unreasonable? I really would like to see Symone, please."

Brayla saw sincerity in Sedric's eyes that she had never seen before. She never realized that Sedric ever felt that way about Symone. She paused and said, "We'll be at Kidz Land at noon. You can meet us there," Brayla said, walking away.

Sedric said, "Thank you," and drove off.

Brayla went in the house, got Symone to leave. They arrived at New Christian Academy, a private performing arts school owned and operated by Nia in the suburbs of

Detroit. They parked and walked into the office for their tour.

"Wow, this is nice mama."

A tour guide walked out to greet them. "Hi, I'm Rob. I'll be giving you a tour. Afterwards, you'll meet in the conference room with our director with any questions you may have. Follow me."

Brayla and Symone walked out the office behind Rob, adoring the architecture. "The décor is beautiful," Brayla commented. "This is a gorgeous facility. So artsy, yes definitely got my girl touches on this one," Brayla said to herself.

Rob showed them all of the classrooms and labs on the first floor as well as the offices of the counselors, cafeteria, school store and dance studio. As their tour continued to the upper level, Symone walked onto the balcony and got a view of the stage and was in awe.

"Someday, I'm going to be performing right there on that stage," she said.

Brayla smiled and said, "You can see yourself on that big stage?"

"Yes, mommy," Symone giggled.

The Scales of Love

Rob took them to the library next and walked around to the computer lab and learning center where tutoring is held. Rob ended the tour and showed them to the conference room to meet with the director, Mrs. Taylor. Brayla asked Symone on the way down, "So what do you think of your new school?"

Symone replied, "I like it mama."

Nia greeted them at the conference room door and welcomed them to have a seat. Brayla began to boast to Nia how impressed she was with the academy and how much Symone loved the auditorium. Nia replied, "Thanks. Do you have any questions I could answer about the program or staff?"

Brayla tells Nia, "I had the opportunity to meet with some of the staff and faculty a few weeks ago and the majority of my questions were answered then. However, I do have a question about your school calendar regarding breaks and recitals."

Nia said, "Sure, go right ahead with your questions."

"Do you resume school the day after the New Year if it falls on a Sunday or the following Tuesday? How many recitals do you typically have within a school year? Is your extended year for the entire school or does it go up to a particular grade?"

Barakah Miller

"Those are great questions Brayla! To answer your first question, If the New Year falls on a weekend, typically we usually start back that following Monday, regardless what day it falls on. The answer for your second question is with our intense program, we try to have at least the standard recitals, which is one in the fall, our holiday/winter recital, and our spring program. We have three additional recitals added for the advanced program. Our extended year is for all grade levels; however, we leave that decision up to the parents/guardian for grades third and under."

"This has been enlightening touring your academy. Symone really likes it. We must be on our way. Thank you for your time. You have been very helpful and congratulations on your new endeavor," Brayla said, preparing to leave.

"Thank you, I'm looking forward to having Symone this fall."

"Me too," Symone said.

Brayla and Symone headed to Kidz Land for lunch. When they arrived, Brayla noticed Sedric was there on time, waiting in the parking lot. Brayla parked and got out. Sedric noticed them walking, but he waited a few minutes before walking in. Brayla and Symone placed their order and got some tokens before finding a booth.

The Scales of Love

Symone said, "Mommy, let's play some games while we wait for our food."

Brayla followed behind Symone into the game area. Fifteen minutes later, their order number was called. They headed back to their table to eat. As they arrived at their table, Sedric walked in and joined them.

"Brayla..."

"Hi, Sedric. Have a seat."

Symone moved over to sit next to Brayla. Brayla said to Symone, "This is Sedric," and leaned down and whispered in her ear, "– the man in the picture.

Symone responded, "Oh. Hi, Sedric!"

Sedric said to Symone, "It's so nice to see you. I haven't seen you in a very long time and you have grown to be a very pretty little girl."

Symone smiled and said, "Thank you. Mommy," Symone continued, "I'm finished. Can we play some more before we leave, please?"

"Sure," Brayla responded. "Can Sedric join you?"

"Yes!"

Sedric followed Symone into the game room while Brayla watched them. Memories of her childhood surfaced as she visualized her father and her interacting weeks before he left. "That's it I have got to tell Bishop! I can't charade this any longer..." They played for about an hour before Brayla walked over and told Symone it was time to go. Sedric asked Brayla if he could take a picture with Symone before leaving. Brayla nodded in approval and took the picture. Brayla smiled because the picture reminded her of the one in the photo album that Symone pointed out.

They gathered their things and walked out to the parking lot. Sedric told Brayla, "Thanks for allowing me time with Symone," as he gave Brayla and Symone both a hug.

"Symone enjoyed your company. Have a safe flight."

Sedric smiled and said, "Thanks Brayla...for everything!"

He walked away, looking at the photo Brayla had taken of him and Symone.

19

Hoop Dreams

Sometimes, the greatest joys come from celebrating each other.

A week later, DJ announced that he would be playing for U of M because he wanted to stay close to home. Brayla and Symone, excited that DJ would be less than an hour away from home, leaped for joy at his announcement. Lonzo and Sasha hugged Brayla, proud of DJ's decision. They all embraced each other as DJ walked toward them. They grabbed and hugged him as well.

Lonzo said, "Man, we are all so very proud of you and your decision."

DJ shook Lonzo's hand as if he had gotten the approval from his father. DJ told Lonzo, "You have been the only father figure I've known all my life. You have no idea what those words mean to me. I'm glad my mom chose you as my Godfather."

Lonzo smiled and patted DJ on the shoulder before he said, "Me too!"

The Scales of Love

They all left and headed to Brayla's for lunch and a little family celebration. Nia and Amerus were already at Brayla's setting up and preparing lunch. As Brayla walked in, her phone chimed. It was Bishop. She opened his text and it read, "Brayla, I've been thinking about what you've said in our last conversation. I know it's been over a week or so since we last communicated. But I've been thinking about life, my life...and what I am doing wrong to have gone through the things I have over this time. Through that thought process, one thing has become apparent. Things I used to do, I can't do no more. In saying that, I'm not just talking about us. I'm talking about a transformation from within. Within me! This includes self-perseverance, self-love and self-rededication. So I don't know what else to say. I love you and I know you love me. Maybe that's part of my issue. You deserve more and she deserves better. Mentally, I don't know where things should stand between us. Our hearts are connected, but is it enough? That's the question I ponder when you ask questions like the one you asked a few weeks ago. So I always want to see you, but I don't know where it will lead or end. So please stop asking questions that I don't have the answer to baby. As far as seeing you baby, I gotta take a college tour with my daughter, but Thursday is good."

Brayla put her phone on silence and exhaled. She became hot and sweaty, knowing she had to tell Bishop soon about Symone. She grabbed a glass of ice water and breathed in and exhaled out to calm her nerves before joining her family again. She smiled and asked Amerus if everything was ready to be served. After getting the green light from Amerus, Brayla informed everyone that they could eat after they prayed over the food. Lonzo said a prayer and they all fellowshipped late into the evening.

DJ and Symone helped Nia and Amerus clean while Brayla saw everyone out. Nia walked in and took a seat in the living room, with Amerus and Brayla joining her moments after.

"Whew, girl it's been a long day," Nia said.

"Yes, it has," Amerus agreed.

"Brayla, what's on your mind?" Nia asked. "I could tell after you walked in you seemed a little distant. What's occupying your thoughts?"

"Nothing Nia," Brayla responded. "I'm okay, just a little tired from all the festivities and work. You know I gave Rico the lead on the new development and he hasn't reported back to me yet on the status. That's not like him. I'ma have to go on site tomorrow and that probably means I'll run into Bishop. I'm just not ready for that. We haven't seen each other or talked in almost two weeks. I'm just not ready to see him. Not now anyway," Brayla said, referring to his last text message.

The Scales of Love

"Girl, you worry too much," Amerus said. "It'll all work out. Remember, it's business and I'm sure everything is fine. Rico probably has attempted to call you at the office, I'm sure. Your staff knows your kids come first and you been here for them and they just didn't want to bother you with all that other stuff," Amerus reassured Brayla.

"I know, but this is different. He has my cell number and he knows I expect that report timely, no matter what!"

"Oh girl, it's 10:45 at night. Let me get my tired self up and go home," Nia blurted. "It's been real. We'll talk tomorrow."

"Me too," Amerus added.

"Thanks for everything, divas!"

Brayla headed to her room, crashed on her bed and said, "Yeah, things are starting to feel different, Bishop." She closed her eyes and dozed off to sleep.

At 4:30 in the morning, Brayla woke up and said her daily prayer. Afterward, she got ready for work so she could get an early start and meet up with Rico and Dennis at the site. Moments later, Brayla said her confession, grabbed her briefcase and purse and headed to her car. Before opening the garage, she sent Bishop a morning inspiration that read, "Good morning baby! I pray all is well and whatever you are challenged with works out for your good. 3 John 1-2."

Barakah Miller

She pressed send and Bishop chimed right back.

"Thanks for the words of encouragement."

20

Love Tested

Sometimes the love you have will be tested. It is through the endurance of the test that your strength is revealed –because only the strong survives!

Brayla arrived at the site and had a briefing with Rico and Dennis. Meanwhile, Michael and Bishop went over the development plans and headed up the stairs of the construction site to get a visual of the actual layout of the blueprints. Michael headed back downstairs to get Jalen while Bishop waited on his return.

The beam gave in and Bishop fell thirty feet from the construction site, knocking him unconscious. Someone called the ambulance and Ken talked to Bishop, hoping he'd respond to his voice. When the ambulance arrived, they put Bishop on the stretcher and took him to the hospital. Brayla turned around at the sound of the ambulance and rushed over to find out what happened.

Ken told her that the beam caved in and that Bishop had fallen.

The Scales of Love

Brayla shouted, "What? No, this cannot be true! How was he? Is he okay? Was he conscious?"

Ken replied, "Brayla, calm down. He was not responsive, but breathing. He might have a concussion and a broken leg. I'm headed to the hospital now. I'll be in touch with you later."

Brayla, now speechless, walked away and cried. Rico stood by her car embracing her before allowing her to drive. He offered to take her to the hospital, but Brayla declined as she thanked Rico and said, "I think it'll be best if I go to the office and wait for Ken to call."

Brayla arrived at the office and Olivia told her that Ken had been trying to reach her, and he left his cell phone number for her to call once she got in. Brayla took Ken's number, ran to her office, closed the door and called Ken.

"Hello Ken, it's Brayla. How is he?"

Ken told Brayla, "Bishop is going to be okay. He suffered a broken leg and he might need surgery on it. He has a bad concussion as well. The doctors are keeping him for a few days for observation. Brayla, he told me to tell you not to worry and that he loves you."

Brayla was comforted by Ken's words from Bishop. As a smile graced her face, a tear drop fell from her cheek. She said, "Thanks Ken," and hung up the phone.

Barakah Miller

Brayla picked up her remote and hit Play on her iPod station. Brayla closed her eyes and said a prayer for Bishop as tears began to flood her eyes. Brayla cried out, "Lord, forgive us for our actions. Please send Bishop home to his babies. They need him!"

Suddenly, Amerus knocked at her office door.

Amerus rushed in and hugged Brayla before saying, "I heard. Rico called your office and Olivia called us. I rushed right over here. Baby girl, I'm so sorry!"

Moments later, Sasha and Nia walked in and hugged Brayla. "Girl," Sasha said, "Is he okay?"

Brayla relayed the message Ken gave her.

Brayla said, "You know, there is a cost for the decisions we make and we are held accountable to God for those actions. I feel so bad. I was right there when it happened. I didn't even know he was there yet."

"Girl, I know you are not blaming yourself for this – it was an accident. It's not your fault," Sasha said.

"I know. I'm not saying it's my fault. It's just...never mind," Brayla said.

Nia asked Brayla if she wanted her to drive her home or if she wanted to get away from the office for a little bit. Brayla replied, "Sure, I could use some fresh air."

The Scales of Love

They all left and headed to the parking lot. Amerus said, "I need to get back to the shop. I'll call you later, Bray."

Sasha said, "I'll be over later Bray to help out with the kids."

Brayla said, "Thanks ladies."

Nia and Brayla drove off. "Nia, I don't know what to do. I can't see him like this and even if I wanted to, what I look like going up there to the hospital?"

Nia said, "Girl, I hate to say it, but I warned you."

"I know and I'm not mad at you for being real. I love him so much that sometimes, it just hurts," Brayla said, crying. "Now this...this has got to be God intervention – really!"

Nia pulled off to the underpass and parked. "Brayla, I know you probably are not going to want to hear this, but I'ma say it anyway. As a woman, I find it offensive that you would ever even consider hooking up with him in the first place knowing he was married. No, wait! Let me finish. I'm not judging you. I just want you to understand the reality of this situation. You of all people know what it feels like to have your man cheating on you. So why would you put yourself on the other side of the fence? I know he pursued you and the word says, 'If a committed man pursues a single woman, he is only deceitfully using her.' Why have you allowed him to use and deceive you all these years? Love?!

Barakah Miller

Love is pure and giving my dear and what he's been feeding you is not love. At least, not the love I know my God approves of. Girl, I'm praying for you and Bishop and my baby Symone. Only God can make the best outcome for this mess."

"What am I supposed to say? I'm so numb right now. I don't know what to think. But you're right. You make a valid point."

"I know I do. Besides, you know how judgmental people are and the first person they blame is the woman without any presumption of tacking any of that guilt on the man for his part. It's always the woman who gets the heat and they behinds get a slap on the wrist. That's what pisses me off. If women would address their trifling piece of a man first instead of the woman, this wouldn't be an issue. Don't get me wrong now. If that happens and it continues, then maybe there should be a conversation--a lady to lady conversation, none of that hood mess. We as women should and need to lift each other up, not put division between us, especially not over a man, honey."

"Alright Mrs. Nia, I don't know what else to say. I'm sorry..."

"Ugh..." Nia chimed in, "Don't be sorry to me. It's Mrs. Nyla who I'm sorry for. I bet she thinks she got the bomb.com of a man, too. If only she knew what he was doing behind her back. I wonder how peachy it really would

The Scales of Love

be. Girl, you only know what he was choosing to share with you about her and their relationship. Only Bishop, Nyla and God knows the truth about that. He could have been feeding you lies all this time. How would you know the truth from his lies anyway? You're on the outside looking halfway in. Wake up Brayla! It's never going to be the way you envisioned it to be. Marriage is just that--till death do them part. You know how the vows go. He has chosen her as his wife, not you. He has chosen her to wear his ring, not you. He has chosen her to wear his last name, not you. He has chosen her to bear his kids, not you. Oh, Brayla. I'm so sorry!"

"Nia, I get it. I get it. Just take me back to the office please!" Brayla yelled.

21

Truth Therapy

Sometimes, the harshest truth comes from the ones we love!

It's been almost two months since Bishop's accident. Brayla has been texting him motivational messages to uplift his spirit. Bishop has been laying low, pondering his accident and the fact that he almost lost his life. He returned to work on light duty, but still worked extended hours until he completed his therapy for his leg.

Brayla texted Bishop to check on him, since she had not seen or spoken to him since his accident.

"Good morning, love! I know you have a lot on your mind and things are a little stressful; however, you need to communicate those things with me. I need to know where your head is at...PERIOD! Silence is not acceptable! It leads me to believe the opposite of our last conversation."

Bishop chimed back, "I've been working twenty hours a day, just haven't had time for anything else. But thank you

The Scales of Love

for the thoughtful messages and I appreciate you for caring."

"Wow!"

Seconds later, Brayla texted Bishop, "You need to stop taking me for granted. I'm not always going to be here."

"I don't take you for granted at all."

Brayla dropped her phone and continued working on some sketches for her boutique. Symone came in her room and jumped on Brayla's bed.

"Hi mommy," Symone said.

Brayla leaned forward and kissed Symone on the forehead, before saying, "Did you have fun at the party?"

"Lots! Mommy, can we go over Godma Sasha's?"

"Sure, go give her a call and see when it's a good time to stop by."

Symone jumped off Brayla's bed and went to call Sasha.

Symone walked back into Brayla's room with Sasha on the phone. She passed Brayla the phone. "Hello."

"Hi Bray! Yes, you can bring my baby by. We're home. You all should come. Plus, the divas will be stopping by later as well."

"It's a date. We'll be by."

It was 8:30 in the evening when Brayla and the kids pulled up in front of Sasha's house. Amerus and Nia were already there. Brayla and the kids walked in the back door.

"Hello my peeps," DJ said.

"Come on in," Lonzo said, as him and DJ headed to the man cave and Symone headed upstairs with the other children. Sasha motioned the ladies to join her outside on the patio.

"So, what's up ladies?" Brayla asked.

"Life!" yelled Amerus. "I've been working so much at the spa that I really haven't had much time to focus on Jason, and he's starting to think I'm not interested."

Brayla said, "I 'ma let the Mrs. Divas handle that one."

"Well," Sasha said, "First of all, you've got to reevaluate if a relationship with Jason is what you really want. And if it is, as I'm sure you do, you have got to start putting some time and effort in."

"That's right," Nia added. "You use a calendar to keep track of your appointments at the spa. Start using that bad boy and pencil Jason in for coffee, lunch, dinner...something! I assure you, he'll start to take notice.

The Scales of Love

But don't tell him you have to check your schedule to see when you can fit him in. That'll really tick him off."

"Okay," Amerus said. "I'ma give that a try."

"Bray," Sasha said, "What is it? I sense you have something to say."

"I do, but I don't want either of you to judge me when I tell you."

"Brayla, we would never do that," Amerus said.

"Well, I've been wanting to tell you for a while about the truth between me and Bishop. I just wasn't ready for your reaction or the comments to follow. But at this point, it really doesn't matter. The truth is about to come out soon anyway, and I want you to hear it from me."

Sasha said, "Bray, what are you saying?"

"Bishop is married and has been our entire relationship," Brayla confessed.

"What?!" Sasha and Amerus yelled.

"Oh so Nia, I guess you've known all along by the way of your reaction," Sasha said.

Nia replied, "I have."

Barakah Miller

"Bray, why didn't you say something? Never mind, that's not even the issue at this point," Sasha said. "Bray, I can't believe this!"

Amerus asked, "When did you find out he was married?"

"I've known all along, but he made it as though – that doesn't matter. It is what it is..."

"That dog!" yelled Sasha. "I just lost my respect for him as for you my friend. You should have known better, Bray. I'm so disappointed in you--as a woman, as my friend, as my sister, and as a wife," Sasha said. "I still love you, but I got to keep it real right now with you."

"Well, since we keepin' it real, it gets worse than that. Symone is Bishop's daughter."

There's silence around the table for a few minutes. Sasha said, "You mean to tell me that my baby is fathered by Bishop?! Brayla! You led us to believe all this time that Sedric was her father..."

"– Hold up!" Brayla yelled as she cut Sasha off. "Y'all assumed Sedric was her father. I never, never said that he was."

"Well, you never said that he wasn't either," Amerus chimed in.

The Scales of Love

"Girl, you done went over and under the grain," Sasha said. "Brayla, do you have any idea what you have gotten yourself into spiritually? Did you know that since he was sleeping with you and his wife that y'all have been passing spirits back and forth? So now, whatever was or is in her is now in you and vice versa. Lord, you got some mess to clean up."

"That's deep," Amerus said.

Sasha said, "Brayla, I can't believe a woman as intelligent as you fell for his mess! Look at you! Girl in case you haven't noticed, you are stunningly beautiful. Way high above his standards obviously since he couldn't respect the vow."

Amerus chimed in, "Girl yes, you are so way out of his league. He overachieved getting in with you, and you allowing it is what makes it even worse."

Sasha concluded, "Men who don't respect their vows are vultures in hibernation, just waiting on their next victim. Shoot, they probably think they're the victim. Girl, we about to pray over this situation right now! Amerus, Nia grab Brayla's hand," Sasha insisted.

Sasha prayed, "Lord we come to you on one accord according to your word. You said where there are two or more standing in agreement, you are here in the midst. Father, we ask right now that you will cover Symone from any and all spiritual weapons that may try to come against her from this union. Father, we ask that you strengthen Nyla for what's to come of this revelation. We ask that you give Brayla the wisdom and discernment in sharing this information with Bishop. Allow her heart to be cleansed and provide her restoration, deliverance, healing and grace. Father, remove all guilt, shame and embarrassment that she may feel or that may try to come against her. Break every chain and soul tie in the name of Jesus! Strengthen her to be your witness to others. Protect her from all hurt, harm or danger that may try to come against her or her dwelling. God, we ask for your peace and that you comfort Brayla and remove all things that are not of you from her being. Lord, we love you and we praise you and give you thanks in all that you are preparing, in your matchless name, amen."

Brayla said, "I love you all so much. You're my sisters and I'm so sorry for disappointing you all with the choices I've made. Please forgive me."

Sasha said, "I accept your apology and I too love you. We'll always be sisters, but this here is gonna take a minute to sink completely in. I want you to meditate on Isaiah 41:10 every day till you tell Bishop the truth and after you tell him, okay?"

"Yes, I will."

"Bray, I love you more than you'll ever know. You're my big sis," Amerus said. "I still look up to you. Shoot, ain't none of us perfect. We got demons, too. We just ain't exposed ours. Seriously, It took a lot of strength for you to get to the point to share this and I appreciate your honesty. Thank you," Amerus said.

"Girl, you already know how I feel. We've already been there, but I love you and you already know we sisters for life," Nia said.

"Well, I guess demons of my past with my father abandoning me just kept showing up and now having to deal with it in reverse with Bishop and Symone, has brought me to a place of re-evaluating my relationships and discovering my worth, needs, and wants. Putting them all in alignment with what God has said about me, not my past. You jewels are the best sisters a woman could pray for...I love ya'll!"

Sasha replied, "Bray, you know we all are here for you, no matter what you've got our support!"

"Thanks Sasha," Brayla replied.

22

Love Therapy

The fruit of the Spirit is love, joy, peace, patience, kindness, goodness, faithfulness, gentleness, and self-control...Gal. 5:22-23

Brayla excused herself and walked into the living room of Lonzo's and Sasha's. She was instantaneously consumed with love in the Spirit as she looked at the pictorial display presented in the living room.

"All this love..." Brayla said to herself. Tears began to fall from her eyes as she reflected over her entire relationship with Bishop. She came to realize that she had totally missed the mark on love and although Bishop may have loved her in his own way, it was not what she needed from him.

"Six and a half years, I loved him. Daddy God, all of me loved all of him. From the moment we began, I loved him. I thought we both knew what we wanted and we agreed to build upon our relationship. How foolish of me to give of myself to a man who didn't deserve me. I compromised so much of me for him and for what? Part of which I convinced myself I was in love. As much as I wanted him to be the one

The Scales of Love

I loved, he wasn't mine to love. But I chose to love him anyway. In the end, he may be a good man and I'm a good woman, but that doesn't mean we're supposed to be together. Sometimes, letting go is like forgiving. It's not for them, but for you. I have to let go for me. I love me more and I'm so in love with love. Bishop doesn't love my love the way I do. For me to move forward, I have to change the way I feel about Bishop in order to make this transition in my life. We have Symone to raise together and I cannot allow any emotional distractions to interfere with any decisions I, or we, make concerning Symone. Six years is a long time to live in a dream and wake up without the one you love. So if it's time to move on for me, I'm ready!"

Lonzo came upstairs and saw Brayla crying in the living room. He approached her with a hug and motioned for her to have a seat.

"You know, I've overheard y'all conversation over the last few months about you and Bishop. Not intentionally, but your voices carry in from the patio window. I love you as my sister, the godmother of my kids, the godfather of your kids, and a man of God. I'm going to give you my perspective from a man's point of view. I'm not condoning anything. I'm not saying he's right or wrong. Girl, don't you realize how stunningly beautiful you are? Any man would be honored to have you. Don't you realize you have options beyond Bishop? I know you're probably tired of hearing that, but you need to get that! I kinda think he overachieved when you allowed him in. Don't get me wrong, he's a cool dude, but just not what I envisioned for my sister. Brayla, you are the whole package. The man who gets your heart won't have to look no more. The way you carry yourself, you don't look like the type of woman to want someone else's man or who would be in love with a man you can't have. You portray yourself as if you chose to be in love, you could have whomever you chose. But I believe when he first met you, he wanted you. He probably thought he couldn't pull you so it became his mission to hook you any way he could because he saw something in you he never seen before, although he was married. I mean that in a good way, not a bad way," Lonzo said, pausing for a moment.

"And when he realized he had you, he didn't know how to keep you. He had to figure out how he was going to balance his life, which consisted of his wife and family, and now you. He took on more than he could chew. You were way too much woman for him and he just wasn't ready for it or in a position to give you what you needed. As a man, there's no doubt in my mind that he wanted to be with you and that he really did love you. I'm saying this based on what I've observed through our gatherings and seeing you both interact. I know he cared for you and if there were doubts in my mind, believe me, Sasha would have told you. However, at the end of the day, this is a married man who goes home to his wife daily without regard to your relationship. No matter how much he told you he loved you,

The Scales of Love

and all that other heartwarming stuff, he's at home with her without the intention of ever leaving her or mentioning you. Babygirl, that's real talk! The best way to align with love when you question it in an intimate relationship is through the word of God, Galatians 5:22-23: 'The fruit of the Spirit is love, joy, peace, patience, kindness, goodness, faithfulness, gentleness, and self-control.' If you model that scripture, through the good and bad, you won't have to worry or question if you're being loved right. That scripture is the foundation for me and Sasha. That's where we go to find balance and to renew our love and strength. We ain't been together 20 plus years based on looks," he said. They both laughed.

"So Bray, don't feel bad. The good is going to come out of this and God will be glorified. I love you sis and I pray something that I said resonated with you."

"Thanks Lonzo! I needed to hear that from a male point of view. You're right in a lot of ways. The thing that gets me the most is that I believed him. I trusted him. I trusted him with my heart, my emotions, my love...us. I just can't get how someone can be so darn sincere and end up being fake at the end of the day. Like our relationship didn't mean anything to him. I just can't believe that's how it really was with us at the end of the day. I've had my few dumb moments, including this one, I must admit. But this one is different. Somewhere in my heart, I just can't believe Bishop wasn't 100 on how he felt about me. My heart won't let me believe otherwise."

"Bray, as a man, I gotta keep it real with you. Yeah, he probably was at home many nights, wanting to be with you, but he couldn't. And yes, he probably was at home with you on his mind. But that's as far as it went. In his mind, he probably thought the distance at some point was more for you than him. Meaning he stayed away to keep from hurting you, but you couldn't see that. He's been with this woman for years. I don't care how much he told you he loved you, how much he romanced you, wined and dined you and all that other heartfelt stuff women like. He wasn't going to walk away from her because he loved you."

"That's deep, but truth when you lay it out like that."

"Girl, free yourself and let that man go! I assure you once you do, your options will be waiting."

"I'm working on that Lonzo. Thanks babes! Tell the girls I'll be out in a few minutes."

"Will do."

Brayla got herself together before reconvening with the girls. She had a drink and conversation before rounding up her kids and leaving.

23

The Truth Comes Out

Withholding the truth may seem the best thing to do at times, but eventually, the truth will come out.

Brayla and the kids arrived home from Lonzo's and Sasha's. Brayla immediately sent Bishop a text message: "Hey, let's talk." She proceeded to get ready for bed.

An hour later, she texted Bishop again, "I know you got my text. Why are you being non-responsive?"

Bishop replied twenty minutes later, "I've been on a college tour with the family. I can't always respond when you want me to. Yeah we're gonna have to have a talk! Things are becoming different."

Brayla chimed right back, "I believe I told you I wanted to talk two weeks ago and you never made time for me. Why does this feel like timing is always for the convenience of you?"

The Scales of Love

Bishop replied, "Brayla, I been thinking about what you said and praying about things. I know I can't be what you need. I'm not gone argue or fight it anymore. I love you so much, but my life takes up too much of me to make anyone else happy but what's around me. I'm tired of disappointing you. So what else is left to do but to let my beautiful butterfly fly? My situation is not changing. It's actually getting better over the years. It's just been hard to let go knowing I love you so much. But what else can we do?"

Brayla chimed back, "Before we have this conversation, we need to talk – face to face!"

"How can I tell you face to face when I can't even find time to get to you? I'm not using any excuses. Do you know where I am today?"

"It's easier to make excuses to avoid effort!"

Brayla walked into Symone's room as the moonlight shined on her face. Brayla stood in the doorway gazing at her daughter, trying to figure out a way to tell her that Bishop was her daddy. DJ walked out of his room and embraced his mother.

"Mom, everything is going to be okay. Me and Uncle Lonzo heard y'all talking through the basement window. Y'all weren't exactly the quietest," DJ said, smiling. "Mom, if they can forgive you and God has already forgiven you, then telling Bishop won't be that hard either. Trust God, mom."

Brayla kissed DJ on the cheek and told him to go back to bed.

"Well Lord, he has a point. I've made up my mind and I'm going to tell Symone in the morning and somehow Bishop...that is when he finds the time," Brayla said to herself. Brayla closed Symone's door and headed back to her room.

Brayla said her prayers and crawled into bed, closed her eyes and said, "Father, give me strength." She quoted Isaiah 41:10, personalizing it for herself though, "Brayla, do not fear, for I am with you. I am your God. Do not be dismayed; for I will strengthen you and help you. I will uphold you with my righteous right hand." Brayla softly said, "Thank you, Lord," before she drifted off to sleep.

The next morning, Brayla went to the kitchen to prepare breakfast. The kids came downstairs for breakfast just as Brayla was setting the food on the table.

"Good morning," they all said to each other as they took their seat at the table.

"How did you sleep, Symone?" Brayla asked.

"Like God's little angel," Symone said with a smile. "And you, mommy?"

The Scales of Love

"I'm rested."

DJ said, "That's good to hear. I was a little concerned that you're not getting enough rest with work and all."

"Baby, no need for you to ever worry about me, I'm fine. Thanks for being so concerned honey."

Brayla said to Symone, "Monie, mommy has something she needs to tell you. I know you have been asking about your daddy. You're a big girl now and I think it's time to tell you the truth of who he is. You remember mama's friend Bishop?"

"Yes," Symone replied.

"Well baby, that's your father," Brayla said, exhaling.

Symone was quiet for a moment before saying, "Mama, why did you wait so long to tell me?"

"Baby, because I had to make sure telling you would not hurt you. I prayed about it and God told mommy it was time for you to know."

"Does he know he's my daddy, mommy?"

"No baby, not yet. But I promise you he will...soon."

"Mommy, may I be excused from the table please?"

"You sure can love," Brayla said, watching Symone head toward her room. Brayla motioned to DJ to follow behind her.

DJ walked into Symone's room and found her crying. Symone looked at DJ, confused, before saying, "After all this time he's been coming over, he never noticed me. Mommy never said anything to me that he was my daddy, and he's been right here all this time."

DJ held Symone and told her, "Mommy never intended for this to hurt you. Some things adults do they do to protect us and when the moment is right, then they tell us what we need to know. You know mother loves you very much and she would never put you in harm's way. That's why it took her so long to tell you. It was all done in love, Monie. And I'm sure just as soon as Bishop finds out, he will love you just as much as mom. So don't cry. God knows best and that's why mom told you today. You're a big girl and I know you might not understand. But trust me, it'll all work out for the good. I promise you."

"I love you, DJ!"

A month later, Brayla still had not heard anything from Bishop. She was at her wits end. Wanting to tell him, but not via text, she became frustrated thinking about it. Her phone chimed and it was Bishop. All of a sudden, now he had something to say. Brayla opened his message and read, "Just thinking about you...I am truly missing you!"

The Scales of Love

Brayla responded, "I know I'm worthy of more than just a 'texts' from you. If that's the only way you feel you can communicate with me, don't bother. I'd much rather hear how you feel than read it!"

A week later, Bishop texted Brayla again, "Can I make love to the woman I dream of. I miss you a lot! All of you baby. Wish I could feel your touch!"

Brayla chimed back, "Where is all this coming from...thought we were done...and still you can't communicate any other way?!"

"I'm lying in bed. It's the easiest way to communicate. I never said I stopped loving you, Bray. That part is still so real. I just hate always disappointing you."

At that moment, Brayla snapped, "You know what Bishop Moore? You are one of the most selfish, self-centered, prideful people I know. You have allowed your conceited arrogance to consume so much of you that you have not even took the time to consider the feelings of others. You are carnal-minded and hypocritical. I'm not saying these things to be mean or out of bitterness, but to convict you in your spirit. Have you once given any thought as to what was so important to me to see you in the first place? Instead of you being selfish and not wanting to deal with it, you assumed it's always a dire need when I tell you we need to talk. Well maybe it is a dire need to me. You ever consider that? Of course not because you were only considering yourself! You just brushed me off and now you think you can romance me with a text and all is forgiven?! Wow, and you have the audacity to say you love me! Love Bishop, real love is shown and expressed. You give of yourself to the one you love. Love doesn't linger in the heart and you don't pursue it for months at a time. If you were so into me, you wouldn't keep putting me in a position for someone else to take me from you. If that part is still so real, why are you there texting me?"

"Oh wow...well I apologize for my heart. If you think it's not relevant, I won't bother you again. And no, I have not had the time to contemplate why you wanted to see me. I guess if you really feel that way about me, there is no point in communicating at all!"

Brayla stared at Bishop's message and with all placidity replied, "For once Bishop, this is not about you. You can take that however you like, but it's the truth babes."

"Ok Bray, I'll meet you later at your house. You don't love me no more, huh?"

The Scales of Love

An hour later, Bishop arrived and Brayla walked him to the living room.

"Okay, what is it you have to say love? I'm listening."

Brayla grabbed Bishop's hand and said, "I don't know whether to be mad at you or to just simply love you. You know, when we first got together, I was hesitant to let you in. And when I did, I shared my heart with you once I felt it was safe for me to do so. You made me feel what we had was special. Now you made me question everything about us. Like regretting I ever told you I was celibate for seven years until we got together. I feel instead of you cherishing that it just only intrigued you more sexually."

"Bray, what? Hold up. I can't believe you're saying this! That is so far from the truth..."

"Can I finish? You mean a lot to me and we have experienced a lot of 'firsts,' but our relationship is over. Your consistency toward me has told me everything I need to know about you and how you feel about me. I'm not interested in casual dating or entertaining the thought of making myself available to accommodate you. As I told you before, you can't and won't keep running in and out of my life. You're either going to be in it or out."

"Why does it have to be all or nothing with you?"

"Because I refuse to have just a piece of love when I can have it all! And if I can't have all of you, I don't want it...I don't want it. You're married, you have a wife and share a family. You have made it very clear where your commitment is and there is no reason to continue to romance and hold on to me when you have no intentions on committing to me. I've allowed you to stay in my life far longer than you were supposed to be, and now it's my time to live my life."

"Wow! Bray, when did..."

Brayla cut him off and said, "Let me finish, please. Bishop, you remember when we first broke up, right before I met Sedric?"

"Yeah?"

"Well," Brayla paused, "I was three months pregnant and we had already broken up and I didn't think we would get back together. I know I should have told you then, but the words you spoke echoed in the back of my mind about the stress thing, so I became timid and afraid to tell you."

Bishop let out a big sigh and said, "I've always known in the back of my mind when we got back together Symone was my daughter. I just never said anything. What happened with the pill thing? I watched you take it?"

"I guess you can't always depend on science. I thought I was safe too, but three months later...so here we are six

The Scales of Love

years later, an abortion, no commitment, broken communication, promises, and trust. The only good thing that came out of this is Symone."

"Wow! I'm so sorry you feel that way. I'm even sorrier for treating you the way I have. I know you really love me. I've always known I could never give you what you deserved. Bray, you are a good woman. I'm sorry for all the disappointments and not being there for you. I hate always disappointing you and I didn't know how to handle it. So I just stayed ghost, hoping you would see my distance was to keep from hurting you, not the other way around. But I see that only made things worse for the both of us. Please forgive me. You're such a beautiful woman and friend. I still want you in my life, but I understand if that's not an option. I'm sorry about the abortion. One of us had to not allow our emotions to overtake us in order to think clearly. A lot of people could have gotten hurt, but I guess now that's irrelevant as we're faced with this again. Bray, why you wait so long to tell me? Dang! I apologize if those words made you afraid to tell me, but Bray you never got to be afraid to tell me anything, ever!"

"The abortion was for you, not me. I can't believe I allowed myself to let you talk me into having it. And you were ghost after that. Wow, I sure have made some bad choices with you. And for what? Love? It's so clear to me that you were only willing to entertain the thought of being with me for your own selfish needs. You knew all along what you were doing. You never showed me any provision, just all words to keep me close enough where you knew you still had me. One thing is clear--you will never jeopardize my heart like that again."

Brayla let out a huge laugh as Bishop said, "What's so funny?" He had an awkward look on his face.

"Nothing, it's just when I told you, I just got this huge feeling of relief. I feel so free now that I've told you. The weight on my shoulders has lifted, that's all. Bishop, you didn't say anything. Why?"

"Because I didn't want to ask a question I was afraid of what the answer would be. That day I came by and saw her for the first time since our separation, there was no doubt in my mind then. I knew, B. I knew! I just had to digest that and figure out what the heck I was gonna do."

"So what now, Bishop?"

"Bray, I figured this is what you wanted to say and I've been praying about it. This changes everything. How am I going to explain this to Nyla?"

"That's not my problem or my issue. My concern is Symone. I've already told her about you and she is waiting on you. So again I ask, what are you going to do?"

"Where is she?"

The Scales of Love

"On the patio with DJ..."

"Well, I'm here. We might as well talk to her now."

Brayla walked onto the patio and called Symone to join her in the living room. She informed Symone before entering that Bishop was there waiting on her. Brayla walked back into the living room with Symone and Bishop reached for Symone. He took her hand and said, "Hello, beautiful! I'm sorry it took so long for us to meet. I can't make up for the time that has passed, but I assure you I won't allow any more time to pass us by. I promise. Now there are some things that I have to take care of, but I'm going to try my hardest to be the best daddy I can be for you."

Symone smiled and said, "I can call you my daddy now?"

"Yes, sweetheart. You can call me your daddy."

Brayla smiled as Symone gave Bishop a hug. She noticed a tear drop fall from Bishop's eye. Brayla sent Symone back outside and told Bishop, "You can be mad at me all you want. I don't care. But when it comes to Symone, let me be very clear. Under no circumstances will I tolerate you not being committed to her. So you need to be sure this is something you can handle because you will not make her feel like an outcast or hype her hopes up over broken promises."

"Brayla, we have chemistry. Six and a half years, to be exact. I would never disrespect you or cause any harm to come on Symone. Although this changes our relationship drastically, I still think the world of you. I just got to get my head on straight and figure out how I'm gonna look Nyla in the eye and tell her I've been in love with another woman all these years and, to make the situation even more complicated, she has my child. This is going to be one of the hardest tasks I've ever had to do and have dreaded to do. But now I don't have a choice. So please just be patient with me as I handle this, please."

"I understand, Bishop. Just don't forget about Symone."

24

Learning to Forgive

Forgiving is the highest form of love; in order to forgive one must possess compassion and humility.

Bishop arrived home an hour after talking with Brayla. He walked in and Nyla was waiting for him in the family room. Bishop took a seat and let out a huge sigh.

Nyla asked, "Are you okay?"

"Yes."

"Now that I know you're okay, where have you been?"

Bishop exhaled and opened his eyes as he prepared to tell Nyla about Symone. "I've been out thinking. I have something I need to tell you Nyla."

"What is it?"

Bishop turned and looked Nyla in her eyes and said, "I've been in a relationship with a woman named Brayla

The Scales of Love

Thompson on and off for the past six years. She told me a few hours ago that her daughter Symone is mine."

Nyla, silent in disbelief but not fully surprised, said, "I knew it. I knew in the back of my mind. The night you met her, you were attracted to her and your relationship was far more than just business. You deceived me…how could you have lied and been so insensitive to me all these years? I asked you repeatedly what was your relationship with her and you looked me in my face and lied to me!"

"Nyla, wait – I didn't lie. When you asked me then, we were not together. I hadn't talked to her in months at that time. I never lied about that."

"But you still didn't come clean on your relationship with her either. I'm not as much in the dark as you like to believe. I know about the abortion. Yes Bishop, I knew and you still continued your relationship with her. Bishop, have you forgotten the vows you committed to me, our family, to us?! How could you jeopardize what we've built? You had unprotected sex multiple times. You put my life in danger for your narcissistic ego! Not only that, the ultimate betrayal, you fathered a child outside of our marriage! Twice! How could you disrespect me and our children like that without any regard to the repercussions of your actions? It is so clear to me right now how selfish and self-centered your actions have been. You've only been consumed with yourself. I'm so disgusted with you right now, I can't stand to look at you!"

"Nyla, wait. I'm sorry!"

"That's the only thing you've said since you walked in the door that we agree on--'you're sorry!' I trusted you to protect me. I trusted you with my heart, my love, our love. This is how you show me what our vows mean to you?! You need to leave. I can't stand having you in my presence right now. If you don't leave, I will."

"Nyla, I want us to work through this. I know at this moment, you don't want to entertain this. But, I do want our marriage and we're gonna have to find a way to include Symone in our family now. I know that's a lot to ask of you now. But please work with me."

"Symone didn't ask to be here. You put an innocent child in the middle of your insecurities without thinking of the possibility of fathering a child with this woman. An innocent child, Bishop! I can assure you that you will provide for her if I have anything to say about it. But I can't talk about this right now. I'm leaving. You fathered a child with another woman and you expect me to say, 'Okay baby, we'll get through this.' I'm not sure what I want from you or even if this is something I can accept and stay with you. What is this, payback? Bishop, I'm out..."

The Scales of Love

Nyla walked out and left Bishop standing by himself in the middle of the family room. Bishop fell to his knees in tears and began to pray and ask God for forgiveness and to help him put his family back together. He apologized for not valuing his wife and honoring their vows, and most certainly, taking advantage of Brayla.

Three months passed between the time Brayla told Bishop about Symone and now. Although they had not communicated since that day, things were great for Brayla and the kids. They were enjoying their last few weeks of summer together before DJ left for college.

One Saturday afternoon, Brayla and the kids were enjoying time by their pool when Brayla's cell phone rang. It was Bishop. Hesitant to answer, she placed the phone up to her ear.

"Hello, it's me. Bishop. I was thinking about stopping by in about a half hour or so. Will you be available?"

"That'll be fine. I'll see you then."

Barakah Miller

Brayla went into the house and changed into something more appropriate for Bishop's visit. Then she headed back out on the patio and pondered what to expect from his visit. Brayla picked up her book of quotes and read, "Apologizing does not always mean you're wrong and the other person is right. It just means you value your relationship more than your ego." The doorbell rang and Brayla answered it, expecting it to be Bishop.

"Bishop, come in. So what's up? How are you?"

"I'm good, considering everything that has taken place. I wanted to talk to you about arranging some time to get Symone."

"That'll be great, but what's your living situation? I can't have my baby around someone who doesn't want her there."

"My marriage is not the greatest at the moment; however, God will prevail. Our relationship on the other hand, Brayla, is strictly about Symone. I want to make that very clear. However, we've got to find a way to remain civil. After all, we are raising her together. I want to make sure the transition for Symone is easy and there is no drama attached with it."

"Bishop, I believe I told you 'we' were over a long time ago before this even came up. I reiterated that the night I told you about Symone. I'm not looking for anything more

The Scales of Love

or less from you than to be a father to Symone," Brayla said sternly.

"And I intend to do that. So where do we start?"

"Well, you tell me how you plan on introducing her in the midst of all this?"

"That's fair," Bishop uttered. "Well, she knows I'm here speaking with you and she has agreed to having Symone over. So I was hoping possibly, if you don't have any plans after church tomorrow, I could stop by and pick Symone up and take her to meet her other family."

"Hmm..." Brayla pondered. "It's only been three months. I'm a little concerned about her being around Nyla. I know this is not easy for her. You have to promise me that Symone will not be the center of any nonsense and you know exactly what I'm talking about. Promise me you will love and treat Symone as the father I've admired you to be over the years and you won't put a difference between her and the other children."

"Bray, you know how I feel about my children. I would never do that to Symone or tolerate anyone else mistreating any of my kids. Come on now, it's still me you're talking to. You should know me better than that when it comes to my kids."

"I think I could do that then. Would you like to see Symone while you're here?"

"Yes, I would actually," Bishop said with great joy.

Brayla walked Bishop outside to the patio where Symone was. Symone ran over and jumped in Bishop's arms and said, "Hi daddy, I've missed you!"

"I've missed you more, baby! Symone, how would you like if daddy came back tomorrow and spent some time with you away from mommy? You know you have a few more brothers and sisters who would like to meet you."

"Oh mommy, could I?"

Brayla shook her head in agreement.

"Okay love, daddy has to go, but I'll be back tomorrow to pick you up after church."

Brayla walked Bishop to the foyer and told him, "Thank you for not forgetting about Symone. She already adores you. Don't let her down. One more thing...I want you to know through all the pain, disappointments, deceit, lies and tears in our relationship, I forgive you for everything! Most importantly, I forgive myself and I release myself from you!

Epilogue

Christ encompasses compassion, love and forgiveness unto us. Who are we not to mimic his ways to those who offend us?

Brayla walked out to the top of her staircase overlooking the foyer. She looked at the front door as a ray of light appeared. She extended her right hand as she heard the quiet, still voice comforting and protecting the little girl that was hurt and abandoned by her father. She felt a release of the little girl as she stood in confidence and forgiveness of her past with her father abandoning her and Bishop.

She realized she had realigned her wants and her worth where she could freely show and give agape love without the fear of rejection, abandonment, or sabotaging her relationships. She knew her turning point was when she had given herself permission to release and heal from her past emotions of rejection, neglect, and abandonment from her father was the moment her transformation began.

Brayla also realized the lack of a relationship with her father and his abrupt departure had played a significant role in her relationships and with Symone. Now she was able to identify and solve the unanswered questions she had struggled with all her life and with her most important romantic relationship with Bishop.

The Scales of Love

She thank God for the revelation and the unconditional love as she moved into her room she heard the quiet, still voice comforting her, saying, "Brayla, do not be afraid. You will not be put to shame. Do not fear disgrace. You will not be humiliated. You will forget the shame of your youth and remember no more the reproach of your widowhood. For your Maker is your husband - do not fear, for I am with you; do not be dismayed, for I am your God. I will strengthen you and help you. I will uphold you with my righteous right hand. For I am the Lord, your God, who takes hold of your right hand and says to you, *"Do not fear; I will help you."* - Isaiah 54: 4-5; 41:10 & 13 (NIV)

What About Me (GOD)

The Levels of True Forgiveness

Indiscretion (sin) is against God and His word. To personally experience true freedom and cleansing, there are **three** levels of forgiveness (and confession) that must take place.

1. When you get revelation (conviction) of the sin (missing the mark/doing wrong), you must first go to God, confess the sin and ask forgiveness. Then, repent (turn away and do not repeat the sin by the strength imparted by God's grace).

2. Then, if it is sin that was committed toward a person, you must ask forgiveness of that person (this can be done in their presence or solely in the presence of God).

3. Finally, we must forgive ourselves for the part we played (there is no more condemnation in Christ). Then, and only then, can we experience supernatural healing, restoration and peace. The taste/desire (for whatever it is) is removed (the soul tie is broken) by God.

5 Things Needed In Order for Your Relationship to Survive

1. Communication (verbal communication!) – No texting, sexting, or social media! You need to hear how each other feels, not read it.

2. Respect toward one another.

3. Honesty: builds trust key component in communicating.

4. Consistency: brings stability which in turns develops loyalty.

5. Prayer: gives you deeper insight into your relationship and allows you to be tuned into God concerning your life partner and yourself.

Consistency brings all of it together from one through five. Consistency is just as powerful as communication and prayer without it, you have nothing!

✶ Remember:

Life & Relationships without substance is like a car without gas...EMPTY!

Final Thoughts from the Author

Today we live in a world where the unforbidden sins of infidelity have become conformity of life, love, and relationships. With today's industry of entertainment (TV, music and movies) glamorizing the adulterous sins of extramarital affairs or the cohabitants of living together without any intention on investing in a commitment, you have to wonder, are they intentional or oblivious to the message they are sending to our youth?

Is infidelity in fact a tactic most often used to escape the harsh reality of buried emotions unaddressed in a relationship? Or is it most often sought after for one's own narcissistic ego to justify one's own selfish needs? Or perhaps it goes deeper beyond that, farther than one might conceive throughout history. The real root of the matter could very well be generational.

If infidelity is in your bloodline, it's being passed down from generation to generation. This could very well be your desire to welcome and/or accept the temptation of infidelity. If you've taken root into the power of insecurity, more than likely, your relationship may suffer. You can take a stand to break the cycle. People need to understand that spirits are real so if you or your significant other is cheating, be prepared for a spiritual battle.

About the Author

Bold, fearless, confident, and authentic are just a few words that set the precedence of author **BARAKAH MILLER**, inspirational & transformational coach.

Unapologetic about whom she is and her journey, Barakah has been transforming and encouraging audiences for over a decade. Her powerful message of encouragement, resilience, perseverance, empowerment, and love & relationships has impacted the lives of adults and teens.

As a Michigan native, Barakah saw her experiences as an opportunity to educate others, especially women and teens. She teaches people worldwide about relationships, love, emotional healing, career choices, networking, and most importantly, self-worth. Miller has been providing education and "edutainment" to youth and women for the last decade through her community service, youth organization, ministry and former magazine publication.

Barakah is the CEO of her own company, *Barakah Unlimited*, which is a training and development company where she is a Speaker and Healing & Relationship Catalyst. The Scales of Love, inspired by personal experiences of her life about relationships, love, commitment, forgiveness and self-discovery lead to wholeness. In her debut book, Miller captures her readers with engaging content and engulfs them in the lives of her characters as they come to life with every turn of the page; leaving her readers with profound, thought-provoking questions and conversation.

Barakah works with women and men through her books, seminars, and trainings. She helps them to get closer, to unify with one another. To live on one page, to have more joy and love in their lives, while pushing past anger, moving into forgiveness, and learning self-discovery.

As a thought leader specializing in 'Life, Love, & Relationships' she has audiences captivated through her courage to conquer the most fearful and unhealthy situations. Her series *'He's Scared, She's Scared...The Silence That Sabotages Relationships'* drew audiences into thought provoking, heated, controversial, & sexy conversation.

Fearlessly, bold, and confident Barakah empowers and transforms the hearts and minds of audiences with her eye-opening transparency and passion that Real Love and Authentic Relationships still exist sending the message "Real Love is Healthy Love!"

To learn more visit www.BarakahMiller.com

I WANT TO HEAR FROM YOU!!!

If this book has made a difference in your life,
I would be delighted to hear about it.

Leave a review on Amazon.com!

BOOK ME TO SPEAK FOR YOUR NEXT EVENT!

For speaking engagements or book signings, log onto:
www.BarakahMiller.com
or send an email to info@barakahmiller.com

MEET ME ON
Twitter @MsRaKyee
Facebook.com/Barakah.Miller
Facebook.com/TheRelationshipCatalyst1
Facebook Group: The Scales of Love
Instagram @MsRaKyee
Tumblr @MsRaKyee

www.ingramcontent.com/pod-product-compliance
Lightning Source LLC
Chambersburg PA
CBHW071910290426
44110CB00013B/1344